Effective Empowerment and Delegation

Developing Management Skills

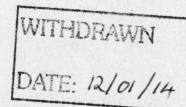

Developing Management Skills

EFFECTIVE EMPOWERMENT AND DELEGATION

David A Whetten
Kim Cameron
Mike Woods

HarperCollins*Publishers*

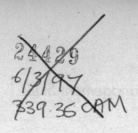

Adaptation (Effective Empowerment and Delegation) copyright © 1996 by HarperCollins Publishers Ltd, UK.

Developing Management Skills 2e, copyright © 1991 by David A. Whetten and Kim S. Cameron.

Adaptation published by arrangement with HarperCollins Publishers, Inc, USA.

This edition first published in 1996 by
HarperCollins College
An imprint of HarperCollins Publishers Ltd, UK
77-85 Fulham Palace Road
Hammersmith
London W6 8JB

British Library Cataloguing in Publication Data. A catalogue record for this book is available from the British Library.

ISBN 0-00-499039-0

Typeset by Dorchester Typesetting Group Ltd
Printed and bound by Scotprint Ltd, Musselburgh
Cover design: The Senate

Other Titles in the Series

Contents

Preface

Effective Empowerment and Delegation is one of a series of six books based on *Developing Management Skills*, a major work by David Whetton, Kim Cameron and Mike Woods. The other titles from this series are *Effective Stress Management*, *Effective Conflict Management*, *Effective Communication*, *Effective Problem-Solving* and *Effective Motivation*. Presented in a convenient form they provide a background of reading and exercises for tutors and students taking MBA grade or other business qualifications.

Each book in the series seeks to find a balance between a sound theoretical background and case studies. Our objective remains, as it did in the combined work, to develop behavioural skills not only to increase knowledge and understanding in the area, but also to assist students to apply what they have learned. We hope our readers will be able to achieve their qualifications **and** become productive members of their organisations by learning applicable skills.

The structure of the books and the method of teaching they employ are, in our opinion unique. Each book begins with a series of questionnaires designed to check on the reader's present understanding of the area, and in some cases assist the reader in self assessment. Thus, in the present book the reader is asked to rate his or her understanding and ability to empower and delegate others.

From these questionnaires the reader will be able to set learning objectives for the book, and on finishing the text, see how much he of she has been able to relate to the very personal world of self.

The main body of the text provides a theoretical background to the issues of empowerment and delegation, and actionable advice on how to tackle these issues. The text closes with two case studies, discussion questions, two empowerment exercises and a section on Application Planning.

Our firm belief is that when 'all is said and done, there is more said than done'. We are asking our readers to make a real commitment to use the material and become more effective in their chosen professions.

Preface

Introduction

The world of the manager has changed significantly since the 1980s. When reorganisation was discussed in the 1980s it was the manager who was doing the reorganising, and the blue collar and clerical staff who were reorganised. Maslow (1965) talked about self-actualisation as a Holy Grail that allowed the individual (the manager) to achieve a personal fulfillment through work. Somehow the 1990s have been different. Charles Handy, from his questioning and optimistic book, *The Age of Unreason* (1990), has moved to his still questioning but profoundly depressing – *The Empty Raincoat* (1994) where he questions whether the professionalism demanded of us, in the new world, is where we want to be going. Herriot and Pemberton (1995) go even further and discuss what they see as a betrayal of contract by organisations, that at its worst leads to industrial sabotage.

The new world, for good or evil, is about professionalism and the new gurus, headed by Hamner (1993), who are concerned with teamwork and empowerment. Empowerment in this new world is less about the 'self actualisation' discussed by Maslow and more about extending the boundaries of Handy's 'inverted doughnut' (1990). It is about increased efficiency, and its output is codified by Handy in the equation:

$$1 \times \tfrac{1}{2} \times 2 = 3$$

Handy is saying that in the new world we take a workforce, divide it by two and facilitate the work of the remaining half so that they can work twice as hard to produce three times the work output. The key word for the facilitation is empowerment and the morality or indeed prudence of such a process is a very hot political issue in current management thinking. Hamner quotes an example from IBM where the same workforce were 'empowered' to produce 100 times the work output.

The case for a move from a dis-empowered workforce is given by the General Motors poem quoted by Peters and Waterman (1982):

> Are these men and women,
> Workers of the World?
> Or is this an outgrown nursery
> with children – goosing, slapping, boys
> giggling, snotty girls?
> What is it about the entrance way,
> these gates to the plant? Is it the
> guards, the showing of your badge – the smell?
> Is there some invisible eye
> that pierces you through and
> transforms your being? Some aura
> or ether, that brain and spirit washes you
> and commands, 'For eight hours
> you shall be different.'
> What is it that instantaneously makes
> a child out of a man?
> Moments before he was a father, a husband,
> an owner of property,
> a voter, a lover, an adult.
> When he spoke at least some listened.
> Salesmen courted his favour. Insurance
> men appealed to his family responsibility
> and by chance the church sought his help . . .
> But that was before he shuffled past the guard,
> climbed the steps, hung up his coat and
> took his place on the line.

Empowerment can couple the enormous potential of mankind by not allowing him (or her) to hand his brains as he (or she) hangs his (or her) coat. It is also, unfortunately, as Herriot and Pemberton have detailed, become an euphemism for downsizing, for sacking people.

> 'You are empowered to make the best and most beautiful grommets in the world.'
> 'I don't want to make grommets – I want to make dreams.'
> 'You're fired!'

Our treatment of empowerment in this book will be optimistic and we will hold the cynics at bay, at least until the next edition.

What we have in this book is a pulling together of all the strands from the other books of these series:

- Empowerment and delegation, although initially stressful, are a powerful way of diminishing **personal stress**.
- **Supportive communication** is essential throughout the empowerment process.
- **Creative problem-solving** is empowering in itself and has to be delegated
- Empowered managers will conflict with their bosses and question the very roots of their organisations – this **conflict needs to be managed**. The manager seeking to empower his or her staff must not see themselves as resolving conflicts – this process has a profoundly dis-empowering effect in itself. However, he or she must be available as a mediator. He or she must also maintain the role of a monitor, holding the empowered individuals and teams on course.

Ken Durham, ex-Chairman of Unilever on meeting new recruits, used to explain his policy on empowerment:

'If you have a dispute with your boss that you cannot resolve – both come to see me. Explain the issues, and one of you will leave this room without a job.'

It was perhaps surprising that very few disputes were left unresolved and very few were referred to him.

We see the current world becoming more and more demanding of managers, and a mastery of the skills of empowerment are fundamental for survival, let alone growth.

Skill Pre-assessment

Diagnostic Surveys for Empowerment and Delegation

Effective Empowerment and Delegation

Instructions

Step 1: Before you read the material in this book, please respond to the following statements by writing a number from the rating scale below in the left-hand column (Pre-assessment). Your answers should reflect your attitudes and behaviour as they are now, not as you would like them to be. Be honest. This instrument is designed to help you discover your level of competence in empowering and delegating so you can tailor your learning to your specific needs. When you have completed the survey, use the Scoring Key at the end of the book (page 83) to identify the skill areas discussed in this book that are most important for you to master.

Step 2: After you have completed the reading and the exercises in this book and as many as you can of the Skill Application assignments at the end of this book, cover up your first set of answers. Then respond to the same statements again, this time in the right-hand column (Post-assessment). When you have completed the survey, use the Scoring Key at the end of the book (page 83) to measure your progress. If your score remains low in specific skill areas, use the behavioural guidelines at the end of the Skill Learning section (page 63) to guide further practice.

Rating Scale

6	Strongly agree	5	Agree	4	Slightly agree
3	Slightly disagree	2	Disagree	1	Strongly disagree

ASSESSMENT

PRE-	POST-	**In situations where I have an opportunity to empower others:**

In situations where I have an opportunity to empower others:

_____ _____ 1. I help people develop personal mastery of their work by involving them first in less complex tasks, and then in more difficult tasks.

_____ _____ 2. I value people by recognising and praising their successes however small.

_____ _____ 3. I try to demonstrate successful task accomplishment.

_____ _____ 4. I point out other successful people who can serve as role models.

_____ _____ 5. I frequently praise, encourage and express approval of other people.

_____ _____ 6. I provide regular feedback and needed support.

_____ _____ 7. I try to foster friendships and informal interaction.

_____ _____ 8. I highlight the important impact that a person's work will have.

_____ _____ 9. I try to provide all the information that people need to accomplish their tasks.

_____ _____ 10. I pass along relevant information to people as I become informed myself.

_____ _____ 11. I ensure that people have the necessary resources – equipment, space and time – to succeed.

_____ _____ 12. If I do not have resources to hand, I help others obtain what they need.

_____ _____ 13. I help people become involved in teams in order to increase their participation.

_____ _____ 14. I let teams make decisions and implement their own recommendations.

_____ _____ 15. I foster confidence by being fair and equitable in my decisions.

_____ _____ 16. I show a personal concern for everyone with whom I have dealings.

When I find I can delegate work to others:

_____ _____ 17. I specify clearly the results I desire.

_____ _____ 18. I specify clearly the level of initiative I want from others (e.g., do part of the task and then report, do the whole task and then report, etc.).

_____ _____ 19. I consult with subordinates on when and how work will be done.

_____ _____ 20. I make certain that the amount of authority and responsibility are in balance when I delegate work.

_____ _____ 21. I work within existing organisational structures when delegating assignments and never by-pass someone without informing him or her.

_____ _____ 22. I identify constraints and limitations people face, but also provide support.

_____ _____ 23. I maintain accountability for results, not for methods used.

_____ _____ 24. I delegate consistently – not just when I'm overloaded.

_____ _____ 25. I avoid upward delegation by asking people to recommend solutions, rather than merely asking for advice or answers when a problem is encountered.

_____ _____ 26. I make clear the consequences of success and failure.

Personal Empowerment Assessment

Instructions

Step 1: This instrument helps identify the extent to which you are empowered in your own work. You should respond to the items based on your own job or on the work you do as a student. The items listed below describe different orientations people can have with respect to their work roles. Use the following scale to indicate the extent to which you believe each is true of you using the Pre-assessment column. Then use the Scoring Key at the end of the book (page 83) to determine the extent to which you are empowered.

Step 2: As in the previous questionaire, after you have completed the reading and exercises in the book, cover up your first set of answers and respond to the same statements again, this time using the Post-assessment column. If your score remains low, use the behavioural guidelines at the end of the Skill Learning section (page 63) to direct you towards areas where further work is needed.

Rating Scale

1 Very strongly disagree 2 Strongly disagree 3 Disagree
4 Neutral   5 Agree   6 Strongly agree
7 Very strongly agree

ASSESSMENT

PRE-	POST-

_____ _____ 1. The work that I do is very important to me.

_____ _____ 2. I am confident about my ability to do my work.

_____ _____ 3. I have significant autonomy in determining how I do my work.

_____ _____ 4. I have a large impact on what happens in my work group.

_____ _____ 5. I trust my co-workers to be completely honest with me.

_____ _____ 6. My work is important to me personally.

_____ _____ 7. My work is well within the scope of my abilities.

_____ _____ 8. I can decide how to go about doing my own work.

_____ _____ 9. I have a great deal of control over what is done in my work group.

_____ _____ 10. I trust my colleagues to share important information with me.

_____ _____ 11. I care about what I do in my work.

_____ _____ 12. I am confident about my capabilities to perform my work.

_____ _____ 13. I have considerable opportunity for independence and freedom in how I do my work.

_____ _____ 14. I have significant influence over what happens in my department.

_____ _____ 15. I trust my co-workers to keep the promises they make.

_____ _____ 16. The work I do is meaningful to me.

_____ _____ 17. I have mastered the skills necessary to do my work.

_____ _____ 18. I have a chance to use personal initiative when carrying out my work.

_____ _____ 19. My opinion counts in departmental decision-making.

_____ _____ 20. I believe that my colleagues care about me and how I am.

Skill Learning

Empowering and Delegating

Books on management skills often concentrate on helping managers to control the behaviour of other people. They focus on how managers can increase the performance of subordinates, engender conformity, or motivate to achieve set objectives.

In the book *Effective Motivation*, we discussed the implications of what is known as the Hawthorne Experiment. In the studies carried out at the Hawthorn Works of General Electric in the 1930s managers appeared to be surprised that a workforce, within a high level of control systems, was able to determine its own work patterns. Our contention is that all workers, whatever the measure of imposed control, at some level, determine their own work patterns and this – if harnessed effectively – is a good thing for them and the organisation.

It is a case of perspective. If we see people determining their work patterns we can either see it as a threat and therefore increase our control, or as an opportunity. In this book we see it as an opportunity and discuss the skills necessary to grasp that opportunity. In the introduction we included the General Motors Poem where it is accepted that workers are capable and competent in their own private lives, and act in a way that meets all our criteria of empowerment; but somehow when they enter the factory door they have to be controlled. Before the 'hanging of the coat' and the simultaneous 'hanging up of the individuality' the organisation has already 'trusted' the worker. Imagine the worker leaving for work. The starting time for duty is set, but the means of getting to the fixed point by the appointed time is normally left to the worker. The myriad of minor decisions that have to be made cannot be usefully proscribed – how to react to children who are slow getting up, to cars that fail to start, to bad weather, to minor ailments and injuries. These not only can be left for the individual to handle, but it would be madness to do otherwise. The manager's job is only to facilitate where necessary and monitor success and failure. In the jargon of this book, workers are empowered at this level because any intervention is accepted as dysfunctional. Empowerment at this stage is accepted, if not remarked upon.

We can ask a further question – what is important, getting to work at a proscribed time or doing the job effectively? Once we ask this question and all the related questions, we are beginning to discuss empowerment and the coincident factor of trust in a meaningful way.

With any job, at some level of activity, tight ruling is impossible. We are arguing in this book that the supreme management skill is finding the HIGHEST level of activity that workers can be left to handle the chaos that is the working environment, and defining a new role of management – the role of facilitator, mentor/guide, monitor and provider of direction.

> James Gleick (Chaos, Abacus, 1987) developed a metaphor in which he sees us operating as a free running ball bearing trapped in a bowl. Within the bowl we use all our native skills to produce order – to establish equilibrium. Using the metaphor, the manager's job is to provide depth to the bowl – a clear definition of task and purpose, energy to keep moving in the bowl – resources and to guard us from spilling out of the bowl.
>
> Mike Woods, using the metaphor in lectures demonstrated the concept using a real metal bowl representing the work situation and a ball bearing representing the individuals or teams within. Passing round the bowl, scratched by the movement of myriad's of ball bearing movements seeking their own equilibrium, the students notice that from any viewpoint, the scratches seem to have an unique focus. So it is, for us, when we are empowered. We feel we are the focus of the activity and this makes us feel good – empowered and motivated.

The empowering manager can leave the demeaning jobs of timing how long people spend in the washroom or how they travel to work, and concentrate on the important issues of cash flow, contributions, product, process and service development. Issues around providing for customers, developing the busines and ensuring that all the stakeholders receive just rewards are the real jobs of managers. Close supervision of peripherals not only degrade the role of the manager and the individuality of the worker but are also downright unproductive. The Hawthorne Experiment has told us that in the 1930s.

Managers who empower people or teams remove controls, constraints and boundaries, and facilitate work – providing resources, stimulating, motivating, steering and most of all creating a world of mutual, but realistic trust. Rather than being a 'push' strategy, in which managers induce employees to respond in desirable ways through incentives and influence techniques, empowerment is a 'pull' strategy. Empowerment focuses on ways that managers can design a working practice to energise and provide a positive atmosphere of encouragement. In such an atmosphere, people accomplish tasks because they want to and not because they are offered a carrot on a stick.

Empowering others, however, can lead to dilemmas. On the one hand, evidence shows that empowered employees are more productive, more satisfied and innovative, and that they create higher-quality products and services than non-empowered employees (Sashkin, 1982, 1984; Kanter, 1983; Greenberger and Stasser, 1991; Spreitzer, 1992). Organisations are more effective when an empowered workforce exists (Conger and Kanungo, 1989; Gecas, 1989; Thomas and Velthouse, 1990). On the other hand, empowerment means giving up control and letting others make decisions, set goals, accomplish results and receive rewards. It means that other people probably will get credit for success. Managers with high needs for power and control (see McClelland, 1975) face a challenge when they are expected to sacrifice their needs for someone else's gain. They may ask themselves: 'Why should others get all the prizes when I am in charge? Why should I allow others to exercise power, and even facilitate their acquiring more power, when I naturally want to receive the rewards and recognition myself?'

Ricardo Semler, in his book *Maverick*, describes what is certainly the most widely publicised example of the empowerment of a whole workforce. Virtually every delegatable authority and responsibility in his

Brazilian company Semco was vested at the lowest level in an already very flat organisation. There is however, a very telling quotation in his book:

'Fernando, THE LAST OF our Attilas, was the first key manager to be expelled by the new Semco. He was very smart and very capable, but unequivocally autocratic.' (Semler, 1993)

Not every manager can take the challenge. The second dilemma is concerned with the definition of control, or perhaps monitoring and control. Empowered teams within workforces may well reach their objectives but the manager, who should be aware of a broader picture, needs to make sure that the objective is and remains the right one. In our explanation of an empowering manager we have used the word 'steering' and we must not forget that steering will always need judgement and on occasion, tough decisions should 'the boat not respond to the tiller'. This issue will be illustrated by the BA Case Study at the end of the book (page 71).

Although empowering others is neither easy nor natural (we are not born knowing how to do it), it need not actually require a great amount of self-sacrifice. A person doesn't need to sacrifice desired rewards, recognition or effectiveness in order to be a skilful empowering manager. On the contrary, through real empowerment, managers actually multiply their own effectiveness and need to broaden their sphere of understanding. They and their organisations become more effective than they could have been otherwise. Nevertheless, for most managers, empowerment is a skill that must be developed and practised, because despite the high visibility of the concept of empowerment in popular literature, its actual practice is all too rare in modern management. McClelland (1975) gives an example of how it can be done, and some of the difficulties. The attitude survey at the end of the article indicates that there is still a long way to go.

While chairmen pronounce their latest vision for their company, more often than not in the bowels of the organisation their instructions are being interpreted, subverted or merely ignored. Alex Krauer, chairman of Ciba, the Swiss chemicals and drugs group, should know. For two years senior managers at the company, which last week reported post-tax profits up 19 per cent, have been struggling to implement a 'cultural revolution'. The revolution's aim is to make the organisation more flexible and responsive by giving its shop-floor employees more responsibility. The scheme, called Vision 2000, is, in current management jargon, all about empowerment.

Krauer explains: 'Everything depends on implementation; this mustn't just be a declaration of intent. We must actively involve every employee in the process. The danger is that we create a level of expectation and then nothing happens.'

The implementation of Ciba's vision has not run smoothly as Heini Lippuner, chief operating officer, admits: 'We do not have a uniform adoption of the leadership style we would like. The causes for the different degrees of implementation are multiple. Partly it depends on the attitudes of the individuals at the top of Ciba's 14 divisions.'

Italy is touted as one of the examples where empowerment has worked. Sergio Giuliani, corporate head of Ciba Italy, says the Italian management during the early 1980s was authoritarian, hierarchical and bureaucratic. 'By definition a successful company becomes complacent and conservative,' he says. Since then, layers of management have been ripped out and a start made in devolving decision-making down the organisation.

But in Basle, at Ciba's headquarters, Lippuner claims that a risk-averse bureaucratic culture still exists: 'There is a passion in Basle for avoiding mistakes. That makes empowerment difficult because personal initiative brings the possibility of making errors. The Swiss character cherishes its traditional ways.'

The company has moved the headquarters of three of its divisions out of Basle in an effort to escape the deadening hand. A fourth, the eyecare division, Ciba-Vision, is relocating to Georgia later this year. At Ciba's pigment division headquarters in Paisley, Scotland, Jean-Luc Schwitzguebal, managing director, says moving divisional headquarters out of Basle is vital: 'Our performance is now our responsibility. We can't blame anyone else. We can't bitch that we are doing everything right, but Basle is screwing it up.'

Krauer identifies a further key component for successful implementation: 'The critical area is middle management. If it stops there, then the whole exercise is wasted. Some fully support the changes, while others are afraid. Others refuse to delegate because they believe that by doing so they lose power.'

Lippuner explains further: 'I meet young people on the shop-floor who tell me they like the vision, they believe we are sincere about empowerment. But they complain that there has been no real change.

To put it pointedly, it looks as though we have a layer of clay that prevents anything going either way – up or down. That layer is middle management.'

The resistance to change is sometimes unconscious, says Giuliani. 'There is often an unspoken contract between boss and employee. They play a game.'

Ciba is putting immense effort into explaining the programme. As Krauer says: 'If you don't understand and don't believe, you won't take on the vision.'

Senior management plans to crack the layer of clay by creating pressure from both above and below, and through education. Questionnaires about superiors' leadership behaviour were sent to the 20,000 employees in Switzerland. The aim, says Krauer, was to set up a level of expectation from employees and use that expectation to force middle managers into dialogue.

Krauer believes 90 per cent of managers are capable of adopting the vision: 'A few, and I hope only a few, will not want to co-operate and they had better look for a job outside Ciba. There is too much at stake for people in key positions not to be part of the process.'

Lippuner says he does not want to paint too black a picture. There have been changes in small units away from Basle where leaders have been particularly dynamic and deployed private initiative. Jim McDonald says he is at the bottom of Ciba. A team leader at Paisley – a plant cited by Lippuner as a success – McDonald says the vision has filtered its way down.

Colin McKay, the boss of his plant, is delighted. He explains how maintenance problems have been resolved by giving workers responsibility.

Attitude surveys at Paisley suggest that nearly 70 per cent of employees are proud to work for Ciba. 'That includes people who spend most of their day shovelling chemicals. They are surprisingly good figures,' says Schwitzguebal who claims Paisley was the only classical pigment producer making money in western Europe last year.

McDonald agrees that management is now far more effective, allowing the possibility of avoiding problems before they happen. But in spite of Paisley's model status, he argues that there are still difficulties. Team leaders wanted to meet to discuss similar issues, but the middle management initially blocked their meetings. 'We should meet one another – we have plenty to talk about,' he says. In the end, permission was given. Elsewhere, employees are also enthusiastic about the changes. At Ciba's epoxy-resin plant in Duxford, Cambridgeshire,

Lionel Webb, customer service centre manager, describes proudly how his department was restructured after employees were polled about the business's problems.

Ciba managers admit the success of the Italian and Paisley businesses cannot be put down just to the vision. For various reasons, the cultural change started earlier still has a long way to go. As Lippuner says: 'I have no illusions about inertia – I've worked in this organisation for 35 years. But that does not mean we will capitulate.'

A recent attitude survey gave the following results in Table 1.

Table 1　Ciba: attitude survey

Over all of Ciba	Strongly agree	Agree	Unsure	Disagree	Strongly disagree
I feel my boss recognises my work's importance	11.1	32.2	16.3	21.3	19.1
I need more training to do my job	17.5	21.6	12.9	29.7	16.5
I feel very much left on my own	15.4	20.3	17.6	30.3	16.5
I enjoy the challenge of my job	23.6	44.8	12.5	10.6	8.5
I feel proud to work for Ciba	22.9	46.4	20.2	5.0	5.6
I can't wait to leave and find a better job	9.3	13.3	14.4	27.0	36.0

Source: *Financial Times*, London, 5 April, 1993.

What is Empowerment?

One of the most well-researched findings in organisation and management science over the last four decades has shown that when environments are predictable and stable, organisations can function as routine, controlled, mechanistic units. Under such conditions, workers can be expected to follow rules and procedures and to engage in standardised, formalised behaviour. Managers can maintain control and issue top-down mandates regarding the strategy and direction to be pursued by the organisation. This is not the way most businesses are today. Emery and Trist (1965) described four stages of organisational climate.

■ **Placid** – an environment where companies can 'graze'. There is plenty of everything for everyone.

■ **Clustered** – where smaller companies are joining together to form 'empires'.

■ **Reactive** – where organisations are looking to optimise their position against others in what is seen to be a relatively static and stable market place.

■ **Turbulent** – where very little can be predicted and the rule is 'decide where you want to be and go for it.'

The modern jargon attached to our present way includes such words as 'hyper-turbulence', 'complexity', 'speed,' 'competition', 'chaotic', 'revolutionary change' suggesting that we are in Emery and Triss' *turbulent environment*. Under such conditions, prescriptions for organisational and management effectiveness call for a flexible, autonomous, entrepreneurial workforce (Peters, 1992; Drucker, 1988), rather than one which relies on management for direction and control. Less centralised decision making, less top-down direction, and less autocratic leadership are all prescribed as prerequisites for high-performing modern organisations.

When environments are unstable and unpredictable – when they change a lot or change in unpredictable ways – organisations must be more flexible and organic. Workers are expected to be adaptable and self-managing. Managers must involve others in decision-making, and facilitate broad participation and accountability (Eisenhart and Galunic 1993; Lawrence and Lorsch, 1967). The flexibility of the workers must match the flexibility of the environment (Ashby, 1956).

Our own research has discovered, however, that instead of becoming adaptable, flexible, autonomous and self-managing, individuals in rapidly-changing, complex environments tend to react in the opposite way. Both managers and employees tend to become less flexible, less adaptable, less autonomous, less self-managing, more stable, more rigid and more defensive when they face turbulence and change (Cameron, Whetten and Kim 1987).

In our research on how organisations are managed when they

face decline, turbulence, a reducing labour force and change, we find one reoccurring factor which inhibits positive change – the 'devil that we know attitude'.

The Devil That We Know

The tendency to prefer the 'devil that we know' in response to change was dubbed 'threat-rigidity' by Staw, Sandelands and Dutton (1981). At the very point when people need to be proactive in facing change, they tend towards the exactly opposite behaviour. They become conservative and defensive relying more than ever on old habits and past behaviours. In reaction to a perceived threat, they do that which they know how to do best, or that which has worked best in the past. Despite new circumstances in which old behaviours may not be effective, there is an escalating commitment to habitual behaviour. People seek fewer options, look for information that confirms their previous biases, and become more narrow-minded in their perspectives. In addition, less communication occurs among workers. When individuals in organisations are divulging information, they become vulnerable by putting their personal expertise or untested ideas at risk. This sense of vulnerability magnifies the feeling of uncertainty brought about by changing conditions. Under such circumstances, people are less likely to become contributing team members and to try out new, innovative ideas. Fear and conflict increase, while trust, morale and productivity decrease. The reactionary mode is typical of most interactions, as loyalty and commitment to the organisation become eroded. The tendency in such circumstances is for most important decisions to be made at the top of the organisational hierarchy, because managers at the top feel an increasing need to be in control and to be closer to decisions. On the other hand, people at lower organisational levels become hesitant to make decisions without getting approval from a superior.

If people become more dependent on top managers in uncertain times rather than more independent, how can we ever foster effective performance? How can we ever expect a workforce in a changing environment to develop the prescribed characteristics for effectiveness – that is, to be adaptable, flexible, autonomous and self-managing?

The answer to these questions is to use empowerment. If managers are empowered themselves and are skilled at empowering their subordinates, the inertia that drives organisations toward dysfunctional 'devil that we know' attitude is counteracted. Workers become more effective, even in the face of trying times. Empowerment is a key to unlocking the potential of a successful workforce in a modern era of chaotic change and escalating competitive conditions.

But what is empowerment? What does it mean to be an empowered worker? What is the set of management skills associated with empowerment?

To empower means to enable; it means to help people develop a sense of self-efficacy; it means to overcome causes of powerlessness or helplessness; it means to energise people to take action; it means to mobilise intrinsic excitement factors in work. It is more than merely giving power to someone. Power does allow us to get things done, but empowerment involves not only the capacity to accomplish a task, but also includes a way of defining oneself. Empowered people not only possess the wherewithal to accomplish something, they also think of themselves differently than they did before they were empowered.

Historical Roots of Empowerment

The word empowerment has been in vogue in the 1980s and 1990s, yet as a concept it is by no means new. The concept of empowerment has been referred to in many books and articles in the last few years, and it has become popular to use the term to refer to everything from team-building to decentralised structures. In fact, the word has been so overused that its precise meaning may have become obscured. It may be helpful, therefore, to provide a brief background of the roots of empowerment. This should help avoid confusing empowerment with other related management behaviours. Empowerment has roots in the disciplines of psychology, sociology and theology, dating back decades – even centuries.

The concept of 'mastery motivation' emphasises the way people strive for competence in dealing with their world. Similar concepts introduced several decades ago include 'effectance motivation', an intrinsic motivation to make things happen (White, 1959); 'psychological reactance', which refers to seeking freedom from constraints (Brehm, 1966); 'competence motivation', a striving to encounter and master challenges (Harter, 1978); and 'personal causation', a drive to experience free agency (DeCharms, 1979). In each of the preceding studies, the root concepts are similar to the notion of empowerment discussed in this book – i.e., the inclination of people to experience self-control, self-importance and self-liberation.

In sociology, notions of empowerment have been fundamental to most 'rights' movements (e.g., Civil Rights, Women's Rights, Gay Rights) – (see Solomon, 1976; Bookman and Morgan, 1988), in which people campaign for freedom and control of their own circumstances. Moreover, much of the writing attacking problems through social change has centred fundamentally on the empowerment of groups of people (Marx, 1844; Alinski, 1971). That is, people seek social change in order to increase their access to an empowered condition.

In theology, debates about free-will versus determinism, self-will versus submissiveness, predestination versus faith and works, and humanism versus positivism have been hotly debated for centuries. At their root, they are all variations on a theme of empowerment versus helplessness. The more recent literature on 'liberation theology' (Friere and Faundez, 1989) emphasises the empowerment of individuals to take charge of their own destinies, rather than relying on the dictates of an all-controlling, supernatural force. This does not mean that people who believe in a Supreme Being cannot feel empowered; rather, it implies that they can couple a sense of self-mastery and self-determination with their faith in a higher power.

Empowerment, then, is not a new concept. It has appeared in various forms throughout modern management literature. In the 1950s, for example, management literature was filled with prescriptions that managers should be friendly to employees (human relations); in the 1960s, that managers should be sensitive to the needs and motivations of people (sensitivity training); in the 1970s, that managers should ask employees for help (employee involvement); and, in the 1980s, that managers should form teams and hold meetings with employees (quality circles) (see Byham, 1991). The continuation of these themes in the 1990s suggests that managers should empower people. But despite the continuing emphasis on various versions of employee involvement and empowerment, the ability to empower employees is still not common in most managers' repertoire of skills. Empowerment is more rarely seen than prescribed.

Inhibitors to Empowerment

In his book on managerial empowerment, Peter Block (1987) noted that empowerment is very difficult to accomplish:

> Many, increasingly aware of the price we pay for too many controls, have had the belief that if some of these controls were removed, a tremendous amount of positive energy in service of the organisation would be released. While in many cases this has happened, too often our attempts at giving people more responsibility have been unwelcome and have met with persistent reluctance. Many managers have tried repeatedly to open the door of participation to their people, only to find them reluctant to walk through it. [In a study of managers who were offered total responsibility for their work areas], about 20 per cent of the managers took the responsibility and ran with it, about 50 per cent of the managers cautiously tested the sincerity of the offer and then over a period of six months began to make their own decisions. The frustrating part of the effort was that the other 30 per cent absolutely refused to take the reins. They clutched tightly to their dependency and continued to complain that top management did not really mean it, that they were not given enough people or resources to do their jobs properly, and that the unique characteristics of their particular location made efforts at participative management unreasonable.

As Block noted, many managers and employees are reluctant to accept empowerment, but they are even more reluctant to *offer* empowerment. One reason for this is the personal attitudes of managers. Several management surveys, for example, have examined the reasons managers have for not being willing to empower their employees (Newman and Warren, 1977; Preston and Zimmerer, 1978; Byham, 1991). These reasons can be organised into three broad categories, as follows.

1. **Attitudes, beliefs and assumptions about subordinates.** Managers who avoid empowering others often believe their subordinates are not competent enough to accomplish the work, aren't interested in taking on more responsibility, are already overloaded and unable to accept more responsibility, would require too much time to train, or shouldn't be involved in tasks or responsibilities typically performed by the boss. They feel that the problem of non-empowerment lies with the employees, not with themselves. The rationale is: 'I'm willing to empower my people, but they just won't accept the responsibility.' They adopt a Theory X stance – (see glossary, page 87).

2. **Personal insecurities.** Some managers fear they will lose the recognition and rewards associated with successful task-accomplishment if they empower others. They are unwilling to share their expertise or 'trade secrets' for fear of losing power or position. They have an intolerance for ambiguity which leads them to feel that they personally must know all the details about projects assigned to them. They prefer working on tasks by themselves rather than getting others involved, or they are unwilling to absorb the costs associated with subordinates making mistakes. The rationale is: 'I'm willing to empower people, but when I do, they either mess things up or try to grab all the glory.'

3. **Need for control.** Non-empowering managers often have a great need to be in charge and to direct and govern what is going on. They presume that an absence of clear direction and goals from the boss, and a slackening of controls will lead to confusion, frustration and failure on the part of employees. They feel that direction from the top is mandatory. Moreover, they often see short-lived, disappointing results from pep talks,

work teams, suggestion systems, job-enrichment programmes and other 'fix-it' activities (i.e., 'We tried that, and it didn't work'). The rationale is: 'I'm willing to empower people, but they require clear directions and a clear set of guidelines; otherwise, the lack of co-ordination leads to confusion.'

The rationale associated with each of these inhibitors may be partially true, but they nevertheless inhibit managers from achieving the success associated with skilful empowerment. Even if managers demonstrate the willingness and courage to empower others, success still requires skilful implementation. Incompetent empowerment can undermine rather than enhance the effectiveness of an organisation and its employees. Such incompetent empowerment as giving employees freedom without clear directions or resources has been found to lead to psychological casualties among individuals, as manifested by increased depression (Alloy *et al* 1984), heightened stress (Averill, 1973), decreased performance and job satisfaction (Greenberger *et al* 1989), lowered alertness and even increased mortality (Langer and Rodin, 1976). Of course, these negative consequences are not solely associated with ineffective empowerment. But they have been noted, nevertheless, in situations where attempted empowerment was ineffective and unskilful. For example, when managers associated empowerment with behaviours such as 'simply letting go', refusing to clarify expectations, abdicating responsibility, having an absence of ground-rules, or giving inflexible or inconsistent directions – none of which are consistent with skilful empowerment – the results were not only unsuccessful, but even harmful. Because of the negative psychological and physiological consequences for workers resulting from non-empowerment or from incompetent empowerment, Sashkin (1984) labelled skilful empowerment 'an ethical imperative' for managers.

Dimensions of Empowerment

In one of the best empirical studies of empowerment to date, Spreitzer (1992) identified four dimensions of empowerment. We have added one dimension to her model, based on the research of

Mishra (1992). In this section, we explain these five key dimensions of empowerment. In order for managers to empower others successfully, they must engender these five qualities in those they intend to empower. Skilful empowerment means producing a sense of:

■ Self-efficacy
■ Self-determination
■ Personal control
■ Meaning
■ Trust in other people

When managers are able to foster these five attributes in others, they have succeeded to empower others. We suggested earlier that empowered people can not only accomplish tasks, but that they also think differently about themselves.

Self-efficacy
When people are empowered, they have a sense of self-efficacy – the feeling that they possess the capability and competence to perform a task successfully. Empowered people not only feel competent, they feel confident that they can perform adequately. They feel a sense of personal mastery, and believe they can learn and grow to meet new challenges (see Bennis and Nanus, 1985; Conger and Kanungo, 1988; Bandura, 1989; Gecas, 1989; Zimmerman, 1990). Some writers believe that this is the most important element in empowerment because having a sense of self-efficacy determines whether people will try and persist in attempting to accomplish a difficult task.

> The strength of people's conviction in their own effectiveness is likely to affect whether they would even try to cope with given situations . . . They get involved in activities and behave assuredly when they judge themselves capable of handling situations that would otherwise be intimidating . . . Efficacy expectations determine how much effort people will expend and how long they will persist in the face of obstacles and adverse experiences (Bandura 1977).

Much research has been done on the consequences of self-efficacy and its opposite, powerlessness, especially in relation to physical and psychological health. For example, self-efficacy has been found to be a significant factor in overcoming phobias and anxieties (Bandura, 1986), alcohol and drug abuse (Seeman and Anderson, 1983), eating disorders (Schneider and Agras, 1985), smoking addiction (DiClemente, 1985) and depression (Seligman, 1975). It has also been associated with an increasing tolerance for pain (Neufeld and Thomas, 1977). Recovery from illness and injury, as well as coping with job loss or disruptions, is more effective and more rapid among people who have developed a strong sense of self-efficacy, because they are more physically and psychologically resilient and are better able to change negative behaviours (Schwalbe and Gecas, 1988; Gecas, Seff and Ray, 1988).

Bandura (1977) suggested that three conditions are necessary for people to feel a sense of self-efficacy: (1) a belief that they have the ability to perform a task, (2) a belief that they are capable of putting in the necessary effort, and (3) a belief that no outside obstacles will prevent them from accomplishing the task. In other words, people feel empowered when they develop a sense of self-efficacy by having a basic level of competence and capability, a willingness to put in effort to accomplish a task, and the absence of overwhelming inhibitors to success.

Self-determination
Empowered people also have a sense of self-determination. Whereas self-efficacy refers to a sense of competence, self-determination refers to feelings of having a choice. 'To be self-determining means to experience a sense of choice in initiating and regulating one's own actions' (Deci, Connell and Ryan, 1989). People feel self-determined when they can voluntarily and intentionally involve themselves in tasks, rather than being forced or prohibited from involvement. Their actions are a consequence of personal freedom and autonomy. Empowered individuals have a sense of responsibility for, and ownership of their activities (Rappaport, Swift and Hess, 1984; Rose and Black, 1985; Staples, 1990; Zimmerman, 1990). They see themselves as proactive self-starters. They are able to take initiative on their own accord, make independent decisions and try out new ideas (Conger and Kanungo, 1988; Thomas and Velthouse, 1990; Vogt and Murrell, 1990). Rather than feeling that their actions are predetermined,

externally controlled or inevitable, they experience themselves as the locus of control.

Research shows that a strong sense of self-determination is associated with less alienation in the work environment (Seeman and Anderson, 1983), more work satisfaction (Organ and Greene, 1974), higher levels of work performance (Anderson, Hellreigel and Slocum, 1977), more entrepreneurial and innovative activity (Hammer and Vardi, 1981), high levels of job involvement (Runyon, 1973) and less job strain (Gennill and Heisler, 1972). In medical research, recovery from severe illness has been found to be associated with having the patient 'reject the traditional passive role and insist on being an active participant in his own therapy' (Gecas, 1989). People who are helped to feel that they can have personal impact on what happens to them, even with regard to the effects of disease, are more likely to experience positive outcomes than those who lack this feeling.

Self-determination is associated most directly with having choices about the methods used to accomplish a task, the amount of effort to be expended, the pace of the work and the time frame in which it is to be accomplished. Empowered individuals have a feeling of ownership for tasks because they can determine how they are accomplished, when they are accomplished and how soon they are completed. Having a choice is the critical component of self-determination.

Personal Control

Empowered people have a sense of personal control over what they do. They believe that they can make a difference by influencing the environment in which they work, the method of working or the work itself. Personal control is 'an individual's beliefs at a given point in time in his or her ability to effect a change in a desired direction' (Greenberger and Stasser, 1989). It is the conviction that through one's own actions, a person can influence what happens. Personal control, then, refers to a perception of impact.

Empowered individuals do not believe that obstacles in the external environment control their actions. Rather, they believe that those obstacles can be controlled. They have a feeling of 'active control' which allows them to bring their environment into alignment with their wishes – as opposed to 'passive control' in which their wishes are brought into alignment with environmental demands (see Rothbaum, Weisz and Snyder, 1982; Rappaport, Swift and Hess, 1984; Zimmerman and Rappaport, 1988; Greenberger and Stasser, 1991; Thomas and Velthouse, 1990). Instead of being reactive to what they see around them, people with a sense of personal control try to maintain command over what they see.

Having a sense of personal control is related to, but distinct from, having power and influence. Power and influence are associated with such things as an individual's position, appearance, skill and visibility. Usually, obtaining power is desirable in order to influence or control the behaviour of others. On the other hand, personal control is focused internally, and the emphasis is on controlling one's own life, space and results. Control of self, more than control of others, is the objective.

Research on personal control suggests that people are intrinsically motivated to seek personal control (White, 1959). They fight to maintain a sense of control of themselves and their situations. Prisoners of war, for example, have been known to refuse to eat certain food, to walk in a certain place or develop secret communication codes, in order to maintain a sense of personal control. A certain amount of personal control is necessary for people to maintain psychological and physical well-being. When people lose personal control over themselves, we usually label them as insane and psychopathic.

Even small losses of personal control can be harmful physically and emotionally. For example, loss of control has been found to lead to depression, stress, anxiety, low morale, loss of productivity, burnout, learned helplessness and even increased death rates (see Langer, 1983; Greenberger and Stasser, 1991). The major predictor of suicide is also the sense of loss of personal control. Having a sense of personal control, then, is necessary for health as well as for empowerment. On the other hand, even the most empowered people are not able to control everything that happens to them. No one is in complete control of his or her life. But empowerment helps people increase the number of personal outcomes that they can control. Often, this is as much a matter of identifying areas in which personal control is possible as it is of manipulating or changing the external environment to increase control.

Meaning

Empowered people have a sense of meaning. They value the purpose or goals of the activity in which they are engaged. Their own ideals and standards are perceived as consistent with what they are doing. The activity 'counts' in their own value system. Empowered individuals believe in and care about what they produce. They invest psychic or spiritual energy in the activity, and they feel a sense of personal significance in their involvement. They experience personal involvement and personal integrity as a result of engaging in the activity (Rappaport, Swift and Hess, 1984; Bennis and Nanus, 1985; Block, 1987; Conger and Kanungo, 1988; Manz and Sims, 1989). Meaningfulness, then, refers to a perception of value.

Activities infused with meaning create a sense of purpose, passion or mission for people. They provide a source of energy and enthusiasm, rather than draining energy and enthusiasm from people. Merely getting paid, or helping an organisation earn money, or just doing a job does not create a sense of meaning for most people. Handy (1994), in his book, *The Empty Raincoat*, regrets that unfortunately he has met many people who are 'empty shells' because they seem to exist entirely for the job. Handy is expressing the hope that we can be something better than mere 'empty raincoats' and instead become associated with something more fundamental, personal, value-laden and, most importantly, more worthy of a human being. It is better perhaps to hope that many people do need to be associated with something more fundamental, personal and more value-laden – i.e. with something more human.

Acquiring personal benefit does not guarantee meaning. For example, service to others may bring no quantifiable personal reward but may be far more meaningful than work that produces a hefty pay-cheque. Involvement in activities without meaning, on the other hand, creates dissonance and annoyance, and produces a sense of disengagement from the work. People become bored or exhausted. Other incentives – such as rules, supervision or extra pay – are required to get people to invest in the work. Unfortunately, these extra incentives are costly to organisations and represent below-the-line expenses that constrain organisational efficiency and effectiveness. It costs companies a lot of money to require work that has little or no meaning to workers. Self-estrangement results from lack of meaning; vigour and stimulation result from meaningful work (see Hackman and Oldham, 1980; Alday and Brief, 1979; Kahn, 1990; Thomas and Velthouse, 1990).

Research into the personal meaning of jobs has found that when individuals engage in work which they feel is meaningful, they are more committed and more involved – they have a higher concentration of energy and are more persistent in pursuing desired goals, they feel more excitement and passion for their work; and they have a greater sense of personal significance and self-worth. Individuals empowered with a sense of meaning also have been found to be more innovative, upwardly influential, and personally effective than those with low-meaning scores (Kanter, 1968; Bramucci, 1977; Nielson, 1986; Deci and Ryan, 1987; Vogt and Murrell, 1990; Spreitzer, 1992).

Trust

Empowered people have a sense of trust. They are confident that they will be treated fairly and equitably. They have an assurance that when they are in subordinate situations, they will not be taken advantage of by those in positions of authority or power. They believe that principles of justice will guide the behaviour of those who control valuable resources (e.g., money, information or time). Even though trust implies being in a position of vulnerability (Zand, 1972), empowered individuals have faith that no harm will come to them (Deutsch, 1973; Luhmann, 1979; Barber, 1983; Mishra, 1992). When they are at the mercy of someone else's decisions, empowered individuals believe that they will not deliberately be injured. Trust, then, refers to a sense of security.

Research has found that trusting individuals are more apt to replace superficiality and facades with directness and intimacy; they are more apt to be open, honest and congruent rather than deceptive or shallow. They are more search-oriented and self-determining, more self-assured and willing to learn. They have a larger capacity for interdependent relationships, and they display a greater degree of co-operation and risk-taking in groups than do those with low trust. Trusting people are more willing to try to get along with others and to be a contributing part of a team. They are also more self-disclosing, more honest in their own communication, and more able to listen carefully to others. They have less resistance to change and are better able to cope with unexpected traumas than are those with low levels of trust. Individuals who trust others are more likely to be trustworthy themselves and to maintain high personal ethical standards (see Gibb and Gibb, 1969; Golembiewski and McConkie, 1975; Mishra, 1992).

Because 'trusting environments allow individuals to unfold and flourish' (Golembiewski and McConkie, 1975), empowerment is closely tied to a sense of trust. Having a feeling that the behaviour of others is consistent and reliable, that information can be held in confidence and that promises will be kept, are all a part of developing a sense of empowerment in people. Trusting others allows people to act in a confident and straightforward manner, without wasting energy on self-protection, trying to uncover hidden agendas, or playing politics. In brief, a sense of trust empowers people to feel secure.

A major issue is concerned with the sense of betrayal that is fostered when a workforce is 'empowered' and then finds that the empowerment is a sham. Herriot and Pemberton (1995) describe the dysfunctional behaviour in terms of:

■ Get out
■ Get safe
■ Get even

They quote examples where the empowerment process had led the workforce to feel that their trust had been betrayed. The most able individuals left the organisation whilst the rest either dug in, taking an extremely conservative approach, or indeed acted as a cancer in the organisation, stopping little short of sabotage. Herriot and Pemberton advocate the linking of empowerment programmes with new formal contracts covering the new working conditions and practices.

Summary
The main point of our discussion has shown that fostering the five attributes of empowerment in individuals produces a positive and productive work environment.
- self-efficacy (a sense of competence)
- self-determination (a sense of choice)
- personal control (a sense of impact)
- meaningfulness (a sense of value)
- trust (a sense of security)

Research findings associated with each of the five dimensions of empowerment indicate that both personal and organisational advantages result when people feel empowered. Negative consequences occur, on the other hand, when people experience the opposite of empowerment – powerlessness, helplessness and alienation. Helping people feel a certain way about themselves and their work helps them to be more effective in the behaviours they display. Some authors have gone so far as to claim that helping others develop this feeling of empowerment is at the very root of managerial effectiveness. Without it, they claim, neither managers nor organisations can be successful in the long term (Kanter, 1983; Bennis and Nanus, 1985; Block, 1987; Conger, 1989). As a psychological state, however, empowerment is never under the complete control of a manager. It is possible for individuals to refuse to feel empowered. However, a sense of empowerment can be influenced significantly by the conditions in which people find themselves. For that reason, the next section of this book discusses specific actions managers can take to empower others.

How to Develop Empowerment

People are most in need of empowerment when they are faced with situations they perceive to be threatening, unclear, overly controlled, coercive or isolating; when they experience inappropriate feelings of dependency or inadequacy; when they feel stifled in their ability to do what they would like to do; when they are uncertain about how to behave; when they feel that some negative consequence is imminent; and when they feel unrewarded and unappreciated.

Ironically, most large organisations engender these kinds of feelings in people, because, as Block (1987) noted, bureaucracy encourages dependency and submission. Rules, routines and traditions define what can be done, stifling and supplanting initiative and discretion. In such circumstances, the formal organisation, not the individual, is the recipient of empowerment. Therefore, in large organisations, empowerment is especially needed but difficult to achieve.

But empowerment is also important outside vast bureaucracies. For example, studies demonstrate positive effects of empowerment on child development, learning in school, coping with personal stress and changing personal habits (see Ozer and Bandura, 1990).

Despite the applicability of empowerment in many different contexts, our discussion focuses on ways in which managers can empower their employees in organisations. We focus on empowerment mainly as a skill needed by managers, even though other people such as parents, teachers, coaches, tutors and friends can also benefit by developing the skills of empowerment.

Research by Kanter (1983), Bandura (1986), Hackman and Oldham (1980) and others has produced at least eight specific prescriptions for fostering empowerment, i.e., producing a sense of competence, choice, impact, value and security. These include:

- Fostering personal mastery
- Modelling
- Providing support
- Creating personal enthusiasm
- Providing necessary information
- Providing necessary resources
- Organising teams
- Creating confidence

Each of these prescriptions is discussed here, some but not all of the advice is similar to that found in the other books of the series, in particular *Effective Communication* and *Effective Motivation*.

This overlap is inevitable and indicates a coherence in the message the authors are attempting to convey.

Fostering Personal Mastery

Bandura (1986) found that the single most important thing a manager can do to empower other people is to help them experience personal mastery over some challenge or problem. By successfully accomplishing a task, defeating an opponent or resolving a problem, people develop a sense of mastery. Personal mastery can be fostered by providing people with the opportunity to accomplish successively more difficult tasks which eventually lead to the accomplishment of desirable goals. The key is to start with easy tasks, then progress by small steps to more difficult tasks until the person experiences a sense of mastery over an entire complex of problems.

Managers can help workers to feel more and more empowered by helping them develop an awareness that they can succeed. One way to do this is by breaking apart large tasks and giving workers only one part at a time. The manager watches for small successes achieved by workers and then highlights and celebrates them. Jobs can be expanded incrementally so that tasks become broader and more complex as workers master their basic elements. Employees are given more problem-solving responsibility as they succeed in resolving more rudimentary difficulties. Managers can also provide opportunities for employees to direct or lead others in a project, task force or committee.

By adopting a soft approach, individuals are given opportunities to succeed in small ways, even though an overall challenge may be formidable (Weick, 1979). Small wins can occur when large problems are divided up into limited units which can be attacked individually. Small wins may seem insignificant by themselves, but they generate a sense of movement, progress and success. When small wins are recognised and celebrated by managers, momentum is generated that leads people to feel empowered and capable.

Lee Iacocca used this strategy to turn around a failing Chrysler Corporation in the early 1980s. An analysis of his speeches to the top management team at Chrysler over a period of five years reveals that even though Chrysler was losing money, costs were too high and quality was a major problem, Iacocca continued to celebrate small successes. For example, he regularly announced that a certain amount of money had been saved, a particular improvement had been produced, or a compliment had been received from a Wall Street analyst – even though the firm was losing a billion dollars a year. A great deal of emphasis was placed on succeeding at small things, all of which were aimed at eventually toppling the much larger challenge of company survival. In this case, continual small wins led to a big achievement.

Modelling

A second way to empower people is to model or demonstrate the correct behaviour that they are to perform. Observing someone else succeed at challenging activities, Bandura (1977) found, provides a forceful impetus for others to believe that they, too, can succeed. It helps people presume that a task is 'do-able', that a job is within their capabilities and that success is possible.

The manager himself may serve as the role model by demonstrating desired behaviours. On the other hand, it may not be possible for a manager to model desired behaviours personally for every single employee he wants to empower. The manager may not see an employee often enough to show him how to accomplish his work, or he may not have time for frequent demonstrations of success. As an alternative, however, managers may be able to draw their employees' attention to other people who have been successful in similar circumstances. They might make it possible for employees to associate with senior or other visible people who could serve as role models, and they could provide opportunities for workers to be coached by these successful people. They can provide employees with mentors who can discuss their own past experiences that were similar to those of the employee.

In other words, empowering people involves making available to them examples of past success. This is consistent with the learning model upon which this book is based. The Skill Analysis step of the learning model exemplifies appropriate and inappropriate behaviour engaged in by others. It provides a model of people who have succeeded in accomplishing the desired skill. This modelling function helps foster a sense of empowerment in individuals who are trying to develop and improve management skills by showing ways in which such skills can be demonstrated successfully.

Think of what happens when a barrier is broken. In track and field athletics, for example, once John Thomas broke the seven-foot high jump barrier and Roger Bannister broke the four-minute mile, a host of other athletes quickly exceeded that standard. But before the first person broke those barriers, they were considered for many years as insurmountable. It took someone to demonstrate that the standard could be exceeded in order for others to experience the empowerment necessary to replicate the accomplishment themselves.

Providing Support

A third technique for helping others experience empowerment is providing them with social and emotional support. If people are to feel empowered, managers should praise them, encourage them, express approval of them, back them and reassure them. Kanter (1983) and Bandura (1986) each found that a crucial part of empowerment is having responsive and supportive managers. Managers seeking to empower their subordinates should find ways to praise their performance regularly. They can write letters or notes to workers, to members of their unit, or even to their family indicating that the employee's good work has been noticed. They can provide feedback to workers about their abilities and competencies. They can arrange for opportunities where workers can receive social support from others by becoming part of a team or social unit. They can express confidence in employees by supervising them less closely, or by allowing longer intervals between the reporting of results. Managers can hold regular ceremonies where recognition is provided for employees' achievements. It may simply be a matter of listening to employees and trying to understand their feelings and point of view.

Managers can empower others, then, by engendering a feeling

that they are accepted, that they are a valued asset, and that they are an integral part of the overall mission or objective of the organisation. This support can be provided either by the manager himself or by co-workers.

Cameron, Freeman and Mishra (1991), described a variety of support activities undertaken by a highly effective manager who was forced to lay off workers due to a cost-reduction exercise by the holding company. The cost reduction exercise forced layoffs and understandably caused trust to be undermined, scepticism to rise and a sense of powerlessness to escalate among employees. Because the announcement came down from the parent company, workers felt that they had lost the ability to control their own destinies. In short, they felt un-empowered.

> The manager held personal meetings with each remaining employee to reaffirm his or her value to the organisation. People were told in a straightforward manner that they were considered to be valuable human resources, not human liabilities. A special 'Build with Pride' week was held in which outsiders – the press, government officials, family members, school classes – were invited to tour the site, and exhibitions allowed individuals to demonstrate special achievements and skills. An impromptu barbecue was held one lunch hour to recognise and celebrate the exceptional efforts of one group of employees. People were assured that counselling, training and assistance would be provided when job assignments changed or positions were merged as a result of the cost-cutting exercise, which was explained in detail. In general, this notable manager attempted to re-empower his workforce by providing social and emotional support in a variety of ways. He helped provide the assistance people needed to cope with the uncertainty resulting from this uncontrollable event. Predictably, both organisational and individual performance results did not deteriorate. Instead, contrary to the general rule performance actually improved.

Creating Personal Enthusiasm

Creating personal enthusiasm means replacing negative emotions such as fear, anxiety or irritability with positive emotions such as excitement and anticipation. To empower people, managers help make the work environment fun and attractive. They make certain that the purpose behind the work is clear. They ensure that people's right brain (the side that controls emotions and passions) is involved in the work as well as their left brain (the side that controls logic and analysis). Bandura (1977) found that the absence of personal enthusiasm (he calls it positive emotional arousal) makes it difficult, if not impossible, for individuals to feel empowered.

Managers need to be very clear about the vision and mission of their organisations. Empowerment without vision leads to chaos. Managers must have a clear picture of what employees are empowered to do and where they are going. This vision and mission must be linked, not only to a desirable future, but also to personal values. Workers must see how what they are doing every day is associated with their basic beliefs. Employees can get more excited about working for the betterment of humankind, for the improvement of the quality of people's lives, and for personal growth and development, than they can for a ten per cent return to institutional investors. This is not to say that revenue for shareholders is unimportant, but it may well be difficult for many people to get enthusiastic about. Managers can also increase workers' sense of empowerment by holding periodic social gatherings to foster friendships among co-workers. In their official communications, they can occasionally include a joke or light-hearted message to relieve tension. They can use superlatives in providing feedback or describing successes (e.g., say 'terrific' instead of 'good'; 'fantastic' instead of 'acceptable'). They can make sure that employees are clear about how their work will affect the company's customers. Managers can schedule regular events where employees can hear compelling motivational messages. They can help identify external threats or challenges that need to be met.

The successful creation of enthusiasm is often associated with athletic teams. Syer and Connolly (1984) in their book, *Sporting Body, Sporting Mind*, explain techniques for 'warming up' sports people which are very similar in principle to those already discussed here for managers. Chuck Coonradt (1985) observed that 'people are willing to pay for the privilege of working harder than they will work when they are paid.' That is, individuals will actually pay money in order to work at a more demanding level than the level at which they work when they are receiving a salary. The following is an example of this.

> The frozen foods industry involves people working in refrigerated warehouses in near-zero temperatures, with both management and the unions attempting to make conditions more bearable. Companies are required to provide insulated clothing and boots, to make hot drinks easily available and to allow ten-minute breaks every hour. In these conditions recruitment is difficult. However, the very same people will dream of a winter holiday in the snow resorts of Austria or Switzerland. They will buy the most expensive equipment, paid for by themselves and once there, they will 'work' very hard with none of the hot-drink vending machines on the slopes or the ten-minute breaks every hour (adapted from Coonradt).

Thus, people actually end up working harder, in worse conditions – and paying for the privilege – than when they are at work getting paid. Why is this so? Why does recreation produce such energy, commitment and sense of empowerment?

Part of the explanation relates to the personal enthusiasm that is a characteristic of many sports. For example, all recreation has a clear goal (e.g., winning, exceeding a personal best). Without a clearly-defined goal, no one gets excited. That goal is always pitted against a standard that people care about (e.g., winning the European Cup, wearing a yellow jersey in the Tour de France, scoring a century against the West Indies). In recreation, the score-keeping and feedback systems are objective, self-administered and continuous. In cricket, for example, everyone knows that if a ball is hit beyond the boundary, it counts as six runs. There is an umpire to make sure that the rules are obeyed and anyone can check on the score at any time. The scoring and feedback systems are one logical explanation of why people enjoy watching sports and athletic events. In recreation, the out-of-bounds is clearly identified. People are aware of the consequence of kicking a soccer ball over the touch-line, of dropping the ball in rugby, or of stepping over the end of the takeoff board in the long jump. They are all out-of-bounds, and everyone knows that out-of-bounds behaviour stops action.

Managers can help empower people through creating

enthusiasm, not just by delivering charismatic speeches and keeping the work climate fun, but also by capitalising on some of the principles of recreation that create excitement – clear goals; objective, self-administered and continuous score-keeping and feedback; and clearly defined out-of-bounds behaviour.

Providing Information

Kanter (1983) identified information as one of the most crucial 'power tools' available to managers. Acquiring information, particularly information that is viewed as central or strategic in an organisation, can be used to build a power base and to make oneself indispensable and influential in that organisation. On the other hand, when managers provide their people with more information instead of keeping it to themselves, those people gain a sense of empowerment and are more likely to work productively, successfully and in harmony with the wishes of the manager. The manager actually enhances his or her power base by involving others in the pursuit of desirable outcomes. With more information, people tend to experience more self-determination, personal control and trust. The resulting sense of empowerment enhances the probability that they will not resist the manager, defend against his or her power, or work at protecting themselves. Rather, they are likely to collaborate with the empowering manager.

Therefore, a manager who wishes to increase an employee's sense of empowerment will make sure that the employee is given all task-relevant information needed to carry out an assignment. The manager will make available, on an ongoing basis, pertinent technical information and data collected by others as it crosses his desk. Managers will keep workers informed about what is happening in other areas of the organisation that might have an impact on what the worker is doing. Managers will keep employees informed of policy-making meetings and senior-level discussions related to their area of responsibility. Workers can be given access to sources closest to the information they need – e.g., senior level people in the organisation, customers or the market research staff. Historical or 'context' information can be shared in order to give the worker as broad a background as possible. Managers should make certain that employees have information about the effects of their own behaviour on others and the organisation's goals.

Of course it is possible to overload people with information and to create anxiety and confusion with too much data. But our experience has been that most people suffer from too little information instead of too much. Furthermore, if the operative term 'relevant information' is applied in this context, overload is less likely to occur. Spreitzer (1992) found, for example, that people who received relevant information about costs, customers and strategy felt significantly more empowered than those who did not. Block (1987) argued:

> Sharing as much information as possible is the opposite of the military notion that only those who 'need to know' should be informed. Our goal is to let people know our plans, ideas and changes as soon as possible. . . . If we are trying to create the mindset that everyone is responsible for the success of this business, then our people need complete information.

Further confirmation of the importance of providing information to enhance empowerment comes from our own research (Cameron, Freeman and Mishra, 1993). In one study, for example, we interviewed Chief Executives of large, well-known companies every six months to assess organisational changes and strategies being used to cope with declining revenues. In one firm, not much progress was being made in improving the financial outlook. The executive was very careful to share information on financial, productivity, cost and climate indicators in the company only with his senior management team. No one else in the firm had access to that information. However, a change of top executive led to a dramatic change in information-sharing policy. The new executive began to provide information to every single employee in the firm who wished it. No data was treated as the sole possession of senior management. The sweepers had the same access as the vice-presidents. The resulting empowerment experienced by employees led to dramatic results. Employee-initiated improvements increased dramatically, morale and commitment surged, and the resulting financial turnaround made the top executive look like a genius. He attributed his success to his willingness to empower employees by sharing the information they needed to improve.

Providing Resources

In addition to providing information, empowerment is also fostered by providing people with other kinds of resources that help them accomplish their tasks. In this sense, managers who empower others act more like defenders in a soccer team than strikers. They are less directors and commanders than they are resource providers (holding the ball in defence and releasing it to their own mid-field players) and obstacle eliminators (stopping the opposing forward line). One of the primary missions of empowering managers, then, is to help others accomplish their objectives.

Managers attempting to enhance employees' empowerment by providing them with needed resources will make certain that workers receive adequate and ongoing training and development experiences. Sufficient technical and administrative support will be provided to ensure success. Managers will provide employees with space, time or equipment that may not be readily available otherwise. They will make sure that workers have access to communication and/or interpersonal networks that will make their jobs easier. Workers can also be given discretion to spend money on, or commit resources to, activities that they think are important.

It is not realistic, of course, to assume that everyone can have everything he desires. Very few successful organisations have excess resources to be distributed at will. On the other hand, the most important resources that empowering managers can provide are those that help people achieve control over their own work and lives – ones that foster a sense of self-efficacy and self-determination. When individuals feel that they have what they need to be successful and that they have the freedom to pursue what they want to accomplish, performance is significantly higher than when these types of resources are not available (Spreitzer, 1992).

One of the best examples of using resources to empower comes from Carl Sewell, one of the most successful car salesmen in the United States, who described his approach to empowerment through providing resources:

> Not many people get to see our service repair shop – our insurance company wants to keep traffic there to a minimum – but those who do always comment on its cleanliness. And, in fact, it's immaculate. Why? Because, while customers rarely see it, our technicians do. They live and work there every day. Where would you like to spend your day – in a place that's dirty or in one that's spotless? But it's more than just aesthetics. If we make the technicians' work environment more professional, more pleasant and more efficient, and if we provide them with the very best equipment and tools, we're going to be able to hire the best technicians. . . . All this gives them another reason for working for us instead of our competition (Sewell, 1990).

One reason Carl Sewell has been so dramatically successful is that he provides each individual with everything he needs to accomplish desired goals. This is true whether Sewell is dealing with mechanics or top salespeople, and whether his company is selling Rovers and BMWs or Hyundais and Fords. And it is not only 'need to have' resources that Sewell provides, but also some 'nice to have' resources. The watchword is: 'Resources lead to empowerment'.

Organising Teams

There is nothing inherently empowering about being a member of a team unless that team is given the opportunity to share information among its members, make its own decisions, generate and select solutions to important problems, and either implement their solutions personally or present them to those who can implement them. Participating on a problem-solving team or a task force is empowering to the degree that people get a chance to do things they couldn't do by themselves. Not only is it easier to participate in, and influence the decisions of a small team (as opposed to an entire department), but also the subsequent influence of the team can be far greater than the influence of a single individual. A sense of empowerment, therefore, comes from participating in the coalition itself.

In addition to the participation advantages of teamwork, empowerment is also associated with three particular characteristics of teams – autonomy, influence and responsibility. Each of these attributes operates at individual and team levels. Empowerment of individuals and the effectiveness of teams are most probable when:

- Individuals have the ability to maintain autonomy over the roles they perform in the team
- The team maintains autonomy over its own functioning and direction
- Individuals can influence others in the team itself, and the team can influence outside agents
- Individuals take responsibility for their own success
- The team takes responsibility for its own success

When teams are formed, they fulfil the empowerment function if they are given a certain amount of autonomy for their own functioning, influence over their own outcomes and responsibility for their own success. Individuals will reap the advantages of participating in an empowered team just because they are members. But they will experience even greater amounts of empowerment if they are able to maintain autonomy in the team, influence with other team members and responsibility for their own success in the team.

A manager who wishes to increase an employee's sense of empowerment through teams, therefore, might consider asking the person to join a team that will tackle an important problem that the organisation faces. The manager can spend time training and coaching the worker on how to perform various roles in the team to facilitate its success (e.g., task roles and facilitating roles). The worker should be assigned to a team in which his speciality or expertise is not the same as that of other team members, so that each person can bring value and insight to the others. The team can be empowered, not only by solving the problem, but also by being allowed to help implement the solution as well. Avoid assigning a superior to lead the team; instead, assign a facilitator who can ensure that all team members participate and reach consensus. Organise cross-functional teams that will permit workers to get acquainted with others they don't know throughout the organisation and to acquire information that will assist them in accomplishing their jobs. Base part of the appraisal and reward system on successful team membership rather than solely on individual task-specific behaviour.

Lawler (1992) identified three types of teams that managers can use to foster a sense of empowerment – suggestion teams, job-involvement teams and high-involvement teams.

- **Suggestion teams** are formed mainly to generate ideas for improvement. Interaction with team members helps generate more ideas than any person would have had alone.
- **Job-involvement teams** include self-managing work teams organised to accomplish tasks. Work is co-ordinated among all members of the team, and team members take responsibility to teach one another their own jobs.
- **High-involvement teams** are organised to affect an entire organisation. They function like semi-independent businesses, and are rewarded on the basis of how well they provide needed products or services to customers.

Managers can select among the three different types of teams, or from all three types, in order to help individuals increase their sense of empowerment through team membership.

Creating Confidence

The final technique for engendering empowerment is to create a sense of confidence among workers in the trustworthiness of the manager. Rather than being on-guard and suspicious of being mistreated, workers are secure in their feeling that the manager and the organisation are honourable. This confidence helps drive out uncertainty, insecurity and ambiguity in the relationships between employees and the manager. Employees don't feel a need to be defensive or cautious.

There are at least two reasons why individuals feel more empowered as they develop greater confidence in their manager. For one thing, the wasteful, unproductive behaviours associated with mistrust and suspicion are avoided. When people distrust one another, they don't listen, they don't communicate clearly, they don't try hard and they don't collaborate. On the other hand, when trust exists, individuals are free to experiment, to learn and to contribute without fear of retribution. Secondly, individuals who are admirable and honourable always create positive energy for others and make them feel more capable. Not without reason do universities trumpet the number of Nobel Prize winners on their faculties, the publications of their staff, the number of outstanding faculty members in their business schools and the notable achievements of their best students. Although other members of the university may have nothing to do with the achievements being publicised, they gain an enhanced self-image and sense of empowerment because they are affiliated to the same organisation. For the same reasons, creating confidence in a manager helps employees develop a sense of empowerment.

In creating such a sense of confidence and trustworthiness, five factors are especially important:

- **Reliability:** managers who wish their employees to develop confidence in them need to exhibit reliability. Their behaviour must be consistent, dependable and stable. Their action must be congruent with their words and attitudes.
- **Fairness:** good managers also need to be fair and not take wrongful advantage of anyone. They are equitable in their actions. Workers are clear about the criteria used by the manager in making judgements, and how the manager applies those criteria. Managers must make clear the standards by which workers will be judged, and ensure that those standards are applied in an unbiased way.
- **Caring:** managers must show a sense of personal concern for workers, and help each one feel that he or she is important to the manager. Managers validate the points of view of their workers, and avoid denigrating them as individuals. When correction is needed, caring managers focus on the mistake or the behaviour, not on the worker's personal characteristics.
- **Openness:** confidence-building managers are open in their relationships. No harmful secrets exist, and relevant

information is shared openly and honestly with employees. This does not mean that a manager cannot keep confidences. But it does mean that workers should not have to worry about hidden agendas that could negatively affect them, because their managers are straightforward and honest.

■ **Competence:** workers need to be made aware of their manager's competence. Employees need to be assured that their manager has the necessary ability and knowledge to perform tasks and to solve problems. Without flaunting their expertise, skilful managers inspire a feeling on the part of employees that their confidence in the expertise and proficiency of their leader is not misplaced.

The power of creating confidence in employees is illustrated by several Chief Executives who were interviewed regarding their keys to successful organisational change. Each executive had managed a reduction of staffing levels or redesign of his organisation, and was attempting to maintain a healthy, productive workforce in the midst of turmoil. The key role of trust and confidence in management is hard to miss (see Cameron, Freeman and Mishra, 1993; Mishra, 1992).

'If they don't believe what I'm telling them, if they think it's all rubbish designed to confuse, don't expect them to go out there and work a little harder. They won't work differently or better. They're not going to be receptive to change unless they understand and trust that the things we're talking about are true. I think trust is the biggest single issue.'

'I had a boss who used to say, 'What you do speaks so much louder than what you say.' I've always kept that in the back of my mind. I believe that. People watch very closely what you do. You cannot underestimate that, you are on trial all the time.'

'What's most important in my organisation is this: being truthful. Tell them what it is – right or wrong or different. Tell them the truth.'

'My people are all 150 per cent dedicated to helping one another. Because nobody can do it alone, they need each other badly. But here comes the openness and trust. You have to talk about those things. I don't think you can go in and accomplish things without talking about what the barriers are going to be in trying to make a change or set a new direction.'

Successful managers create confidence in themselves among their employees. They are authentic, honourable and trustworthy.

Review of Empowerment Principles

The actions we have suggested to increase empowerment are not all relevant in every circumstance or with every person, of course, but developing the skill of empowerment is at least partly dependent on knowing what alternatives are available. Our list is not comprehensive; other activities may be equally effective in empowering people. But the eight prescriptions and the suggestions associated with each of them represent actions that you will want to practise as you try to improve your competence in the skill of empowerment. The Skill Practice section of this book (page 71) provides an opportunity for you to do so.

Research has found that those who are empowered themselves are most inclined to empower others. For that reason, we included a Pre-assessment instrument at the beginning of this book that assesses the extent to which you experience empowerment in your own work. Your scores on the instrument entitled Personal Empowerment Assessment (page 83) indicate how much your own work is empowering for you in terms of self-efficacy, self-determination, personal control, meaning and trust. Knowing what provides a sense of empowerment for you can be helpful as you consider ways in which you, in turn, can empower others. The other instrument that you completed in the Skill Pre-assessment section – Effective Empowerment and Delegation (page 83) – identifies the extent to which you behave in ways that empower people with whom you work and the extent to which you delegate work effectively. How much you actually engage in the behaviours discussed above is assessed, as well as the extent to which you are an effective delegator. It is to the topic of delegation that we now turn.

Delegating Work

Empowerment is most needed when other people must become involved to accomplish the task. Obviously, if a person is doing a task alone, knowing how to empower others is largely irrelevant. On the other hand, it is impossible for a manager to perform all the work needed to carry out an organisation's mission, so work and the responsibility to carry it out must be delegated to others. All managers, therefore, are required to empower their employees if they are to accomplish the tasks of the organisation. Without delegation and the empowerment that must accompany it, no organisation and no manager can succeed in the long term. Delegation involves the assignment of work to other people, and it is an activity inherently associated with all managerial positions. In this section, we discuss the nature of delegation as well as ways in which delegation can be most effectively empowering. Delegation normally refers to the assignment of a task: it is work-focused. Empowerment, on the other hand, is focused on individuals' feelings: it relates to the way people think about themselves. We have previously discussed ways in which managers can affect people's sense of being empowered. We shall now discuss ways in which managers can get work accomplished effectively through *empowered delegation*.

We begin by pointing out that although delegation is commonly practised by managers, it is by no means always competently performed. In fact, one of the grand masters of management, Lester Urwick (1944), claimed that the 'lack of courage to delegate properly, and of knowledge of how to do it, is one of the most general causes of failure in organisations.' Moreover, as pointed out by Leana (1987), researchers have paid little attention to delegation, and less is known about the relationships between delegation and management effectiveness than about many other common management skills (Locke and Schweiger, 1979).

Advantages of Empowered Delegation

Learning to become a competent delegator who can simultaneously empower others has several important advantages for managers. It obviously helps managers accomplish more work than they could accomplish otherwise, and can be used as a time-management tool to free up discretionary time. On the other hand, if delegation occurs only when managers are overloaded, those receiving the delegated tasks may feel resentful and sense that they are being treated only as objects to meet the managers' ends. In such cases, they will experience a sense of dis-empowerment. However, skilful use of empowered delegation can provide significant benefits to organisations, managers and individuals receiving assigned tasks.

Empowered delegation can help develop the capabilities and knowledge of subordinates so that their effectiveness is increased. As such, it can be a technique to encourage personal mastery. Delegation can also be used to demonstrate trust and confidence in the person receiving the assignment. Mishra (1992) and Gambetta (1988) summarised research showing that individuals who felt trusted by their managers were significantly more effective than those who didn't feel trusted. Empowered delegation can be used to enhance the commitment of individuals receiving work. Beginning with the classic study of participation by Coch and French (1948), research has consistently demonstrated a positive relationship between having an opportunity to participate in work and subsequent satisfaction, productivity, commitment, acceptance of change, and desire for more work. Empowered delegation can also be used to improve the quality of decision-making by bringing to bear more information, closer to the source of the problem, than the manager has alone. Delegating tasks to those who have direct access to relevant information can enhance efficiency (i.e., require less time and fewer resources) as well as effectiveness (i.e., result in a better decision). Finally, empowered delegation can increase the co-ordination and integration of work by funnelling information and final accountability through a single source. Empowering managers, in other words, can ensure that no cross-purposes occur in delegation and that different tasks are not producing contradictory effects. Competently administered, empowered delegation can produce all five dimensions of empowerment – a sense of competence, choice, impact, value and security.

On the other hand, when delegation is ineffectively performed, several negative consequences can result that not only inhibit empowerment but also subvert the ability to get work accomplished at all. For example, instead of freeing up time, ineffective delegation may require even more time to supervise, evaluate, correct and arbitrate disagreements among employees. Employees may find themselves spending a longer time to accomplish a task because of lack of know-how, experience or information. Stress levels and interpersonal conflict may increase when tasks, accountability or expectations are unclear. Managers may find themselves out of touch with what is really going on with employees, may lose control, and may find goals being pursued that are incompatible with the rest of the organisation. Chaos rather than co-ordination can result. Subordinates may also begin to expect that they should be involved in all decisions and that any decision made by the manager alone is autocratic and unfair.

In the next section, we identify ways in which the positive outcomes of delegation can be cultivated and the potential negative outcomes of poor delegation can be avoided. Of necessity, empowerment and delegation must be linked to the accomplishment of work. We will present guidelines for deciding when to delegate, to whom to delegate, and finally, how to delegate.

Deciding When to Delegate

Empowered delegation involves deciding, first of all, when to delegate tasks to others and when to perform them oneself. When should subordinates be assigned to design and perform work or make decisions? To determine when delegation is most appropriate, managers should ask five basic questions (Vroom and Yetton, 1973; Vroom and Jago, 1974). Studies have shown that when delegation occurred based on these criteria, successful results were almost four times more likely than when these criteria were not followed or considered. These criteria are equally applicable whether assigned work is to be delegated to a team or to a single subordinate.

1. **Do subordinates have the necessary (or superior) information or expertise?** In many cases, subordinates may actually be better qualified than their managers to make decisions and perform tasks because they are more familiar with customer

preferences, hidden costs, work processes, etc., due to being closer to actual day-to-day operations.

2. **Is the commitment of subordinates critical to successful implementation?** Participation in the decision-making process increases commitment to the final decision. When employees have some latitude in performing a task (i.e., what work they do, and how and when they do it), they generally must be involved in the decision-making process to ensure their co-operation. Whereas participation usually will increase the time required to make a decision, it will substantially decrease the time required to implement it.

3. **Will subordinates' capabilities be expanded by this assignment?** Delegation can quickly get a bad name in a work team if it is viewed as a mechanism used by the boss to get rid of undesirable tasks. Therefore, delegation should be consistent (not just when overloads occur). It should reflect an overall management philosophy emphasising employee development. Enhancing the abilities and interests of subordinates should be a central motive in delegating tasks.

4. **Do subordinates share with management and each other common values and perspectives?** If subordinates do not share a similar point of view with one another and with their manager, unacceptable solutions, inappropriate means, and outright errors may be perpetuated. In turn, this produces a need for closer supervision and frequent monitoring. Articulating a clear mission and objective for subordinates is crucial. In particular, managers must be clear about why the work is to be done. Coonradt (1985) found that important people are always told why, but less important people are merely told what, how or when. Telling subordinates why the work is meaningful creates a common perspective.

5. **Is there sufficient time to do an effective job of delegating?** It takes time to save time. To avoid misunderstanding, managers must spend sufficient time explaining the task and discussing acceptable procedures and options. Time must be available for adequate training, for questions and answers, and for opportunities to check on progress.

Empowered delegation depends on a positive answer to each of the above criteria. If any of these conditions is not present when delegation is being considered, the probability is greater that it will not be effective. More time will be required, lower quality will result, more frustration will be experienced and less empowerment will occur. However, a negative answer to any of the above questions does not necessarily mean that effective delegation is forever precluded, because managers can change situations so that subordinates get more information, develop common perspectives, have adequate time to receive delegation, etc.

Deciding to Whom to Delegate

Having decided to delegate a task, managers must then decide whether to involve only a single individual or a team of subordinates. If the decision is made to form a team, it is also important to decide how much authority to give the members of the team. For example, managers should decide if the team will only investigate the problem and explore alternatives, or if they will make the final decision. Managers must also decide whether or not they will participate in the team's deliberations. Figure 1 (next page) presents an analytical framework for helping managers decide who should receive delegated tasks – individuals or teams – and whether the manager should be an active participant in a team if it is formed.

Figure 1 is constructed as a 'tree diagram' that allows a manager to ask questions and, as a result of the answer to each question, move along a path until a final alternative is selected (Huber 1980, Vroom and Jago, 1974). Here is how it works.

If you are a manager determining whether to involve others in accomplishing a task or making a decision, you should look over the considerations below the question, 'Should I involve others in the task or the decision?' If you decide that subordinates do not possess relevant information or skills, that their acceptance is not important, that no personal development can occur for members of the team, that time is tight, or that conflicts will arise among subordinates, you should answer 'no' to this question. The tree then prescribes that you perform the task or make the decision

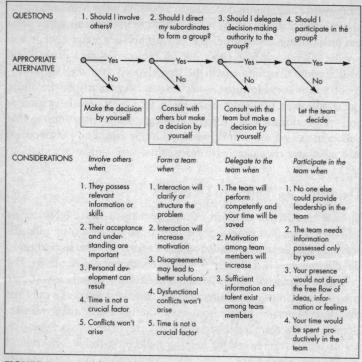

QUESTIONS	1. Should I involve others?	2. Should I direct my subordinates to form a group?	3. Should I delegate decision-making authority to the group?	4. Should I participate in the group?
APPROPRIATE ALTERNATIVE	Yes →	Yes →	Yes →	Yes →
	No ↓	No ↓	No ↓	No ↓
	Make the decision by yourself	Consult with others but make a decision by yourself	Consult with the team but make a decision by yourself	Let the team decide

CONSIDERATIONS	Involve others when	Form a team when	Delegate to the team when	Participate in the team when
	1. They possess relevant information or skills	1. Interaction will clarify or structure the problem	1. The team will perform competently and your time will be saved	1. No one else could provide leadership in the team
	2. Their acceptance and understanding are important	2. Interaction will increase motivation	2. Motivation among team members will increase	2. The team needs information possessed only by you
	3. Personal development can result	3. Disagreements may lead to better solutions	3. Sufficient information and talent exist among team members	3. Your presence would not disrupt the free flow of ideas, information or feelings
	4. Time is not a crucial factor	4. Dysfunctional conflicts won't arise		4. Your time would be spent productively in the team
	5. Conflicts won't arise	5. Time is not a crucial factor		

FIGURE 1 A model for deciding when to delegate to an individual or to a team

yourself. However, if you answer 'yes' to this question, you then move on to the next question: 'Should I direct my subordinates to form a team?' Look over the five considerations below that question and continue through the model. Any of the considerations below a question can result in a 'no' answer. The most participative and empowering alternative is to delegate work to a team and then participate as an equal member of the team. The least empowering response, of course, is to do the work yourself.

Deciding How to Delegate Effectively

When a decision has been made to delegate a task, and the appropriate recipients of the delegation have been identified, empowered delegation has just begun. Positive outcomes of empowered delegation are contingent upon managers following ten proven principles throughout the process, as follows.

1. Begin with the end in mind

Managers must articulate clearly the desired results intended from the delegated task. Being clear about what is to be accomplished and why it is important is a necessary prerequisite for empowered delegation. In fact, unless people know why a task is important and what is to be achieved by performing it, they are unlikely to act at all. No voluntary action ever persists unless these two elements are present. We don't stick with work, school, assignments or other activities unless we have an idea of the purposes and intended outcomes involved. At a minimum, recipients of delegation will infer or fabricate a purpose or desired outcome, or the task will not be performed at all. To ensure that the ends desired by a manager are likewise perceived as desirable by others, the manager should point out the personal benefits to be achieved, the connection of task-accomplishment to the organisation's mission, or the important values represented by the task (e.g., service, learning, growth).

2. Delegate completely

In addition to the desired ends, managers must clearly specify the constraints under which the tasks will be performed. Every organisation has rules and procedures, resource constraints or boundaries that limit the kind of action that can be taken. These should be made clear at the time the task is delegated. In particular, managers must be clear about deadlines and the time-frame for reporting back. When should the task be completed, who should receive the report and to whom is accountability being assigned? No empowerment can occur without knowing what these boundaries are.

Managers also must specify precisely the *level of initiative* expected. No other oversight in the delegation process causes more confusion than the failure to delineate clearly expectations regarding the level of initiative expected or permitted. At least five levels of initiative are possible, each of which may vary in terms of the amount of empowerment available to subordinates. These initiative levels differ in terms of the amount of control permitted over the timing and content of the delegated task:

- **Wait to be told what to do.** Take action only after specific directions are given. This is the least empowering form of delegation because it permits no initiative on the part of the subordinate. There is no control over timing, i.e., when the task is to be accomplished; or content, i.e., what is to be done.
- **Ask what to do.** Some discretion is provided to subordinates in that they have some control over the timing of the task, but not its content. Subordinates may formulate ideas for approaching the task, but because no action can be taken until the manager gives approval, empowerment is highly constrained.
- **Recommend, then take action.** This alternative is more empowering because subordinates are given some freedom over both the timing and the content of the delegated task. However, at least three different types of recommendations are possible, each with a different level of empowerment, as follows:
  - the subordinates simply gather information, present it to the manager, and let him decide what needs to be done
  - the subordinates determine alternative courses of action for each part of the task, leaving the manager to choose which course will be followed
  - the subordinates outline a course of action for accomplishing the entire task and have the whole package approved at once

Progressively more empowerment is associated with each of the following two recommendation types.

- **Act, then report results immediately.** Subordinates are given the freedom to act on their own initiative, but they are required to report to the manager immediately upon completion to ensure that their actions are correct and compatible with other organisational work. Subordinates may be permitted to perform only one part of a task at a time, reporting the results of each individual step. Or, they may be given the discretion to perform the entire task, reporting only when the final result has been accomplished. The latter alternative, of course, is the most empowering, but may not be possible unless the necessary ability, information experience, or maturity is present in the subordinates.

■ **Initiate action and report only routinely.** Subordinates are given complete control over timing and content of the tasks assigned. Reporting occurs only in a routine fashion to maintain co-ordination. With sufficient ability, information, experience and maturity among subordinates, this level of initiative is not only the most empowering, but is also the most likely to produce high satisfaction and motivation among subordinates (Hackman and Oldham, 1980).

The important point for managers to remember is that they must be very clear about which of these levels of initiative they expect of their subordinates.

3. Allow participation in the delegation of assignments
Subordinates are more likely to accept delegated tasks willingly, perform them competently, and experience empowerment when they help decide what tasks are to be delegated to them and when. Often, it is not possible to give subordinates complete choice about such matters, but providing opportunities to decide when tasks will be completed, how accountability will be determined, when work will begin, or what methods and resources will be used in task-accomplishment increases empowerment. Such participation should not be manipulative, that is, opportunities for participation should not be provided merely to convince subordinates of decisions already made. Rather, managers should promote participation when task requirements allow it and when acceptance and personal development can result.

Bernard (1938) formulated an 'acceptance theory of authority' in which he proposed that people will accept and fulfil assignments only if four conditions are met. Subordinates must:
1. Understand what they are being asked to do
2. Perceive that the assignment is consistent with the purpose of the organisation

3. Believe that the assignment is compatible with their own interests
4. Be able to perform the assignment

Bernard's theory underscores the importance of two-way communication during the delegation process. Not only should subordinates be encouraged to ask questions and seek information regarding delegated assignments, but they should also feel free to express ideas about the parameters of the work to be delegated. Expecting subordinates to seek answers to questions, or providing guidance on every aspect of the delegated assignment can perpetuate over-dependence if the manager answers every detailed question or provides continual advice. On the other hand, managers who remain available for consultation and idea interchange, foster two-way communication, and encourage a climate of openness and sharing, make the delegation process empowering.

4. Establish parity between authority and responsibility

The oldest and most general rule of thumb in delegation is to match the amount of responsibility given with the amount of authority provided. It is common for managers to assign responsibility for work to subordinates without furnishing a corresponding amount of discretion to make decisions and authority to implement those decisions. If subordinates are to be successful, they must have as much authority as they need to accomplish the tasks assigned to them. An important part of developing a sense of self-determination and a sense of personal control – both critical dimensions of empowerment – is ensuring this match. Of course, managers also must take care not to delegate more authority than responsibility, thereby giving subordinates more authority, discretion, resources or information than they can use. Such a mismatch leads to lack of accountability, potential abuses of power and confusion on the part of subordinates. For example, without the necessary responsibility, providing a child with a loaded gun, or a £20 note in a sweet shop could result in actions that would not lead to desirable outcomes.

Although managers cannot delegate ultimate accountability for delegated tasks, they can delegate prime accountability. This means that 'the buck stops', eventually, at the manager's desk. Final blame for failure cannot be given away. This is ultimate accountability. On the other hand, managers can delegate prime accountability, which means that subordinates can be given responsibility for producing desired short-term results. Their accountability is to the manager who delegated to them. Giving subordinates prime accountability is an important part of empowered delegation.

5. Work within the organisational structure
Another general rule of empowered delegation is to delegate to the lowest organisational level at which a job can be done. The people who are closest to the actual work being performed or the decision being made should be involved. They are usually the ones with the largest, most accurate fund of information. By definition, this increases efficiency (lower labour and information collection costs), and it frequently increases effectiveness (better understanding of problems). Whereas managers have a broader overall view of problems, the detailed knowledge needed to accomplish many tasks is most likely to reside with those who are lower in the organisational hierarchy.

In delegating a task down more than one level in an organisation, it is important that the organisational chain of command be followed. In other words, delegation must occur through subordinates, not around them. If a senior manager circumvents the formal hierarchy, bypassing a manager to communicate directly with that manager's subordinate, the manager becomes un-empowered. The subordinate now becomes accountable to the senior manager, not the manager with direct responsibility for the subordinate. The entire accountability system is destroyed. Therefore, following the chain of command by involving those at affected levels of the hierarchy in delegation is important for empowered delegation.

All individuals affected by a decision must be informed that it has been delegated. This applies to cross-functional coordination as well as hierarchical coordination. If a subordinate has been delegated responsibility, others who may have needed information, who may influence the results, or who may implement the recommendations must be notified of the delegation. If delegation occurs but no one knows, authority is essentially nullified.

6. Provide adequate support for delegated tasks

When authority is delegated to subordinates, managers must provide as much support to them as possible. As discussed above, this involves making public announcements and presenting clearly-stated expectations. It also involves continuously providing relevant information and resources to help subordinates accomplish tasks. Reports, recent clippings, customer data, articles and even random thoughts that pertain to the delegated task should be passed on as they become available. This support not only aids task-accomplishment but also communicates interest and concern for subordinates. Managers should help subordinates learn where to acquire needed resources, since the manager himself cannot be the sole source of all the support that subordinates will need.

Agreeing on the limits of resource use is also important. Since unlimited access to resources is never possible, managers must be clear about the limit beyond which no further resources can be used. Formulating a budget or establishing a set of specifications is a common way to specify limits.

Another form of support that managers can provide is to bestow credit – but not blame – publicly. Even though prime accountability has been delegated, pointing out mistakes or faults in front of others embarrasses workers, creates defensiveness, fosters the impression that the manager is trying to pass the blame and get rid of final accountability, and guarantees that workers will be less willing to initiate action on their own in the future. Correcting mistakes, criticising work and providing negative feedback on task-performance of subordinates should be done in private, where the probability of problem-solving and training can be enhanced.

7. Focus accountability on results

Once tasks are delegated and authority is provided, managers generally should avoid closely monitoring the way in which subordinates accomplish tasks. Excessive supervision of methods destroys the five dimensions of empowerment: self-efficacy, self-determination,

personal control, meaningfulness and trust. Successful accomplishment of a task, after all, is the primary goal of delegation, rather
than use of the manager's preferred procedures. To be sure, harmful or unethical means for accomplishing tasks cannot be tolerated,
nor can methods be used that obstruct other employees or subvert
organisational rules. But for the most part, managers should focus
their attention primarily on results achieved by subordinates,
rather than on the techniques used to achieve those results.

In order for accountability to be maintained, there must be
agreement on acceptable levels of performance. Managers must
clearly specify what level of performance is expected, what con-
stitutes unacceptable performance, and what requirements are
associated with the result. Without such clearly understood specifications, it becomes difficult for managers not to worry about
means as well as ends. By allowing subordinates to exercise initiative regarding how to tackle a task, their sense of empowerment is
enhanced, and innovation and originality are more likely as well.

8. Delegate consistently

The time for managers to delegate is before they have to. Sometimes, when managers have time to do work themselves, they do just
that – even though that work could and should be delegated. Two
problems result. First, delegation becomes simply a method for
relieving the manager's workload and stress. A primary reason for
delegation – empowering subordinates – is forgotten. Employees
begin to feel that they are merely 'pressure valves' for managers –
useful only for reducing stress – rather than valued team members.

Secondly, when delegation occurs only under pressure, there is
no time for training, providing needed information or engaging in
two-way discussions. Clarity of task-assignments may be impaired.
Workers' mistakes and failures increase, and managers are tempted
to perform tasks alone in order to ensure quality. When managers
delay delegating until they are overloaded, they create pressure on
themselves to perform delegatable tasks personally, thereby
increasing their own overload.

Another key to consistent delegation is for managers to delegate
both pleasant and unpleasant tasks. Sometimes managers keep for

themselves the tasks they like to perform and pass less desirable work along to subordinates. It is easy to see the detrimental consequences this has on morale, motivation and performance. When individuals feel that they are being used only to perform 'dirty work', success completion of delegated tasks is less likely. On the other hand, managers must not be afraid to share difficult or unpleasant tasks with subordinates. Playing the role of martyr by refusing to involve others in disagreeable tasks or drudgery creates unrealistic expectations for employees and isolates managers. Consistency of delegation, then, means that managers delegate tasks continuously, not just when overworked, and that they delegate both pleasant and unpleasant tasks.

9. Avoid upward delegation
Although it is very important for subordinates to participate in the delegation process in order to become empowered, managers must conscientiously resist all so-called 'upward delegation', in which subordinates seek to shift responsibility for delegated tasks back onto the shoulders of the superior who did the initial delegating. Managers who fail to forestall upward delegation will find their time being used to do subordinates' work rather than their own.

Suppose a worker comes to a manager after delegation has occurred and says, 'We have a problem. This job just isn't turning out very well. What do you suggest I do?' If the manager replies, 'I'm not sure. Let me think about it and I'll get back to you,' the original delegated task has now been shifted from the employee back to the manager. Note that the manager has promised to report to the employee, i.e., to maintain prime accountability, and the employee is now in a position to follow up on the manager's commitment, i.e., supervising the manager. Thus, the subordinate has become the manager and the manager the subordinate.

Managers, in the hope of being helpful to, and supportive of their subordinates, often get caught in the trap of upward delegation. One way to avoid upward delegation is to insist that workers always take the initiative for developing their own solutions. Instead of promising the subordinate a report on the manager's deliberations, a more appropriate response would have been,

'What do you recommend?' or 'What alternatives do you think we should consider?' Rather than sharing problems and asking for advice, subordinates should be required to share proposed solutions or to ask permission to implement them. Managers should refuse to solve delegated tasks. That is why specifying the expected level of initiative (see rule 2 above) is so important. Not only does this avoid upward delegation, but it also helps managers train employees to become competent problem-solvers and to avoid working on tasks for which someone else has prime account-ability. Yielding to upward delegation does not empower subordi-nates, but makes them more dependent.

10. Clarify consequences

Subordinates should be made aware of the consequences of the tasks being delegated to them. They are more likely to accept del-egation and be motivated to take initiative if it is clear what the rewards for success will be, what the opportunities might be, what the impact on the ultimate customer or the organisation's mission can be, and so on. In particular, managers should help employees understand the connection between successful performance and financial rewards, opportunities for advancement, learning and developmental opportunities, informal recognition, etc. Most spe-cific delegated assignments do not result in a direct payoff from the formal reward system, of course, but associating some desir-able consequence (such as minor as a pat on the back or a congrat-ulatory mention in a staff meeting, or as major as a financial bonus or incentive) enhances successful delegation.

Clarifying consequences also can help ensure an understanding that delegation not only implies task accomplishment, but an en-hancement of interpersonal relationships as well. Relationships with others in the organisation, in the team, or with the manager individ-ually should be strengthened as a result of task-accomplishment. Accomplishing assignments while damaging or destroying rela-tionships creates more long-term costs than any organisation can bear. Therefore, a desirable consequence of any delegation experience is the enhancement of interpersonal relationships and a strengthening of the organisation.

Review of Delegation Principles

The ten principles summarising how to delegate, preceded by the five criteria for determining when to delegate, and the four questions for identifying to whom to delegate, provide guidelines for ensuring not only that subordinates will experience a sense of empowerment, but also that other positive consequences will result. In particular, research results clearly show that empowered delegation leads to the following consequences:

1. Delegated tasks are readily accepted by subordinates
2. Delegated tasks are successfully completed
3. Morale and motivation remain high
4. Workers' problem-solving abilities are increased
5. Managers have more discretionary time
6. Interpersonal relationships are strengthened
7. Organisational co-ordination and efficiency are enhanced

Summary

Empowerment means helping to develop in others a sense of self-efficacy, self-determinism, personal control, meaning and trust. The current business environment is not particularly compatible with the principles of managerial empowerment. Because of the turbulent, complex, competitive circumstances that many organisations face, managers frequently experience a tendency to be less, rather than more, empowering. When managers feel threatened, they become rigid and seek more control over their employees, not less. However, without empowered employees, organisations cannot succeed in the long run. Learning how to be a competent empowering manager is therefore a critical skill for individuals who probably will face a predilection not to practise empowerment.

Eight prescriptions that managers can use to empower others were discussed. We also offered a series of principles and criteria for ensuring empowered delegation, which results in better acceptance of delegated tasks by subordinates, enhanced motivation and morale, improved co-ordination and efficiency, better development of subordinates, increased discretionary time, strengthened relationships and successful task-performance. Producing a sense of empowerment in others and delegating in a way that empowers subordinates also produces desirable outcomes for organisations as well as employees. Empowered employees are more productive, psychologically and physically healthy, proactive and innovative, persistent in work, trustworthy, interpersonally effective, intrinsically motivated, and have higher morale and commitment than employees who are not empowered.

Behavioural Guidelines

Empowerment

As you practise empowering others and carry out empowered delegating, you will want to use the following guidelines as cues. To ensure empowerment in others:

1. Foster personal mastery experiences for others by:
- Breaking apart large tasks and helping the person do one part at a time
- Involving people in simple tasks before difficult tasks
- Highlighting and celebrating small wins that others accomplish
- Incrementally expanding the job responsibilities of others
- Giving increasingly more responsibility to others to solve problems

2. Successfully model the behaviours you want others to achieve by:
- Demonstrating successful task-accomplishment
- Pointing out other people who have succeeded at the same task
- Facilitating interaction with other people who can serve as role models
- Finding a coach or tutor for the person
- Establishing a mentor relationship with the person

3. Provide needed support to other people by:
- Praising, encouraging, expressing approval for, and reassuring others when they perform well
- Writing letters or notes of praise to employees, as well as to their family members and co-workers, in recognition of noteworthy accomplishments
- Providing regular feedback to people
- Fostering informal social activities in order to build cohesion among people
- Supervising less closely and providing more time between reports on results
- Holding formal and informal recognition ceremonies

4. Arouse positive emotions among others by:
- Fostering activities to encourage formation of friendships
- Periodically sending light-hearted messages to people to keep the climate fun and interesting
- Using superlatives in giving positive feedback
- Highlighting compatibility between important personal values held by your employees and the organisation's goals
- Clarifying the impact of outcomes on ultimate customers
- Fostering attributes of recreation in work by making goals clear, instituting effective score-keeping and feedback systems, and specifying out-of-bounds behaviour

5. Provide information needed by others to accomplish their work by:
- Providing all information relating to the accomplishment of a task
- Continuously providing technical information and objective data that may come to you from time to time
- Passing along relevant cross-unit and cross-functional information to which others may not have access
- Providing access to information or to people with senior responsibility in the organisation
- Providing access to first-hand rather than second-hand information
- Clarifying the effects of employees' actions on customers

6. Provide resources needed for others to accomplish their work by:
- Providing training and development experiences or information about where they can be obtained
- Providing technical and administrative support or information about where they can be obtained
- Providing needed time, space, equipment or information about where they can be obtained
- Ensuring access to relevant information networks
- Providing discretion to others to commit resources that will help accomplish ultimate objectives

7. Involve others in teams and task forces by:
- Assigning a team an important task or problem
- Letting a team not only solve a problem but implement the solution as well
- Assigning facilitators instead of leaders to the team, in order to foster equal participation and involvement
- Fostering information-sharing and learning among team members

■ Basing reward systems at least partly on effective team member-ship, not just on individual performance
■ Helping team members teach and develop one another

8. Create confidence among others by:
■ Being reliable and consistent in your behaviour toward others
■ Being fair and equitable in all your decisions and judgements
■ Exhibiting caring and personal concern for others
■ Being open and honest in your communications
■ Exhibiting competence and expertise with regard to objectives to be achieved

Delegation

To effectively achieve empowered delegation:
9. Determine when to delegate work to others by addressing the fol-lowing six key criteria:
■ Do subordinates have the information or expertise necessary to perform a task? Are they closer to the relevant information than you are?
■ Is the commitment of subordinates critical to successful implementation?
■ Can subordinates subvert task accomplishment?
■ Will subordinates' capabilities be expanded by this assignment? Will it help others to develop themselves?
■ Do subordinates share a set of common values and perspectives? Are there likely to be conflicting points of view?
■ Does sufficient time exist to do an effective job of delegating? Can adequate information and training be provided?

10. Determine to whom work should be delegated by using the deci-sion tree in Figure 1 (page 52). Decide whether you should do the task yourself, consult with individual subordinates, consult with a team of subordinates, or participate as an equal member of a team of subordinates by analysing the characteristics of the subor-dinates.

11. To delegate work effectively, follow these ten rules of thumb:
■ Begin with the end in mind; specify desired results
■ Delegate completely; identify the level of initiative to be taken by subordinates
■ Allow participation, especially regarding how and when tasks will be accomplished

- Match levels of authority with levels of responsibility; maintain balance
- Work within the structure; when delegating work at lower levels, delegate through subordinates, not around them
- Provide support for tasks being delegated; identify resource limitations
- Maintain accountability for results; avoid overly close monitoring of methods
- Delegate consistently; do not delegate merely because you are overloaded
- Avoid upward delegation; ask subordinates to recommend solutions rather than asking for assistance or advice
- Clarify consequences; identify important effects of successful task-accomplishment

Skill Analysis

Cases Involving Empowerment and Delegation

Minding the Store

On 1 January, Claire Cummings was formally named branch manager for a regional super store. On her first day, her boss, Ken Harris said 'Claire, I'm putting you in charge of this store. Your job will be to run it so that it becomes one of the best stores in the group. I have a lot of faith in you, so don't let me down.'

One of the first things Claire did was to take on an administrative assistant to handle stock levels. Because this was such an important part of the job, she agreed to pay her assistant slightly more than some of her assistant managers. She felt that having an administrative assistant would free her to handle marketing, sales and personnel matters – areas she felt were crucial if the store was to be a success.

Within the week, however, she received a call from Harris: 'Claire, I heard that you have taken on an administrator. Do you think this is a good idea? Besides, I hear you are paying him over the odds. That could be bad for morale, don't you think? I wish you had cleared this with me before you made the move. It sets a bad precedent for the other stores, and it makes me look like I don't know what is going on in the branches.'

Three weeks later, Claire appeared on local radio to discuss new trends in fashion. She had worked hard to make contact with the hosts of the show, and she felt that public exposure like this would increase the visibility of her store. Although the interview lasted only ten minutes, she was pleased with her performance and with the chance to get public exposure.

Later that night at home, she received another phone call from Harris: 'Don't you know the policy of the group? Any radio or TV appearances have to be cleared through Head Office. We like to have you showing initiative but it is normally better to leave that sort of thing to the PR people. It's too bad that you didn't tell me first – the whole thing is a trifle embarrassing.'

Just before Easter, Claire was approached in the store by one of the sales clerks. A customer had asked for credit on approximately £1,000 worth of china as a gift for his wife. He had been a customer of the store for several years and Claire had seen him on several occasions, but store rules indicated that no credit could be given more than £500 for any reason. She told the customer that she was not authorised to agree the full sum but would check it out with Head Office and see if special arrangements could be made.

Later in the day, an irate Harris called again: 'What in the world are you thinking about, Claire? Today we had a customer come into the main store and say that you wouldn't make a sale to him because the charge was too much. Do you know how long he has been a customer of ours? And do you know how much he spends in the store every year? I certainly hope we have not lost him as a customer because of your blunder. This makes me very upset. You've just got to learn to use your head.'

Claire thought about the conversation for several days and finally decided that she needed to see Ken Harris. She called his secretary to arrange an appointment for the following day.

Discussion Questions

1. What rules-of-thumb related to empowerment were violated by Ken Harris? By Claire Cummings?
2. What rules-of-thumb related to delegation were violated by Ken Harris? By Claire Cummings?
3. What should Claire Cummings and Ken Harris discuss in their meeting? Identify specific agenda items that should be raised.
4. What are the questions that Claire should ask Ken to help her acquire the necessary elements of empowerment? What questions should Ken ask Claire in order to be better able to ensure her success?
5. If you were an outside consultant attending the meeting, what advice would you give Ken? What advice would you give Claire?

Changing the Portfolio

You are head of a staff unit reporting to the Finance Director. He has asked you to provide a report on the firm's current portfolio, including recommendations for changes in the selection criteria currently employed. Doubts have been raised about the efficiency of the existing system given the current market conditions, and there is considerable dissatisfaction with prevailing rates of return.

You plan to write the report, but at the moment you are perplexed about the approach to take. Your own speciality is the bond market and it is clear to you that detailed knowledge of the equity market, which you lack, would greatly enhance the value of the report. Fortunately, four members of your staff are specialists in different segments of the equity market. Together, they possess a vast amount of knowledge about the intricacies of investment. However, they seldom agree on the best way to achieve anything when it comes to investment philosophy and strategy.

You have six weeks before the report is due. You have already begun to familiarise yourself with the firm's current portfolio and have been provided by management with a specific set of constraints that any portfolio must satisfy. Your immediate problem is to come up with some alternatives to the firm's present practices and to select the most promising for detailed analysis in your report.

Discussion Questions

1. Should this decision be made by you alone? Why, or why not?
2. If you answered the question 'Should I involve others?' affirmatively, which alternative in Figure 1 (page 52) should be used in making a decision? Justify your choice.
3. What are the most important considerations in deciding whom to involve in this task?
4. If others are to become involved, how much empowerment should they have? What would you do specifically to achieve the appropriate level of empowerment?

Skill Practice

Exercises on Empowerment
British Airways

At the beginning of the 1980s British Airways (BA) was in trouble. The growing deregulation of international air traffic meant air fares were no longer fixed and the resulting price war hit BA hard. At the same time it was beset by internal problems. The merger of British Overseas Airways (BOAC) and British European Airways (BEA) had left the airline overstaffed, it had a bureaucratic style of management, there were damaging industrial disputes and its customer service was poor. By 1981–2 it was losing money rapidly.

That was when Margaret Thatcher's government decided to cut its losses and privatise the airline. In order to sell BA shares on the stock market it was necessary to make BA profitable. Lord King, a senior British industrialist, was appointed chairman and he embarked on a survival plan.

Staff numbers were cut from 60,000 to 38,000 by a combination of voluntary severance and natural wastage. Unprofitable routes were abandoned. Surplus assets, particularly aircraft, were sold off and within two years BA was back in profit.

But to ensure long-term success there had to be a fundamental shift in the way BA did business. The airline had to change from being operationally-driven to being market-led. Shortly after he was appointed Chief Executive in February 1983, Colin Marshall described the organisation as one that '. . . didn't really understand the word profit, that was fearful of moving into the private sector, that was quite demoralised.'

The appointment of Marshall represented a significant departure from BA culture. An outsider to BA, Marshall had a marketing background that was quite different from many of his predecessors, many of whom were retired senior Royal Air Force officers.

It was Marshall who decided, shortly after his arrival, that BA's strategy should be to become 'the World's Favourite Airline'. Without question, critical ingredients in the success of the overall change were Marshall's vision, the clarity of his understanding that BA's culture needed to be changed in order to carry out that vision and his strong leadership of that change effort.

Marshall's direct style of management energised the 'unfreezing' stage of the change process. His senior managers were given specific goals and he cut through the traditional 'management by committee' approach. Training had been a casualty of the early 1980s, a trend which Marshall quickly reversed. He saw the need to 'create some motivational vehicle with the employees so that we had a better prospect of raising their morale and in turn seeing better customer service flow.'

Extensive market research had revealed a gulf between customer and staff expectations of the delivery of service. This set the direction for the first of the company-wide, culture-change interventions under the campaign banner of 'Putting the Customer First – if we don't someone else will.'

An ambitious corporate event, 'Putting People First' (PPF), was launched in November 1983. It focused on the idea that 'if you feel OK about yourself you are more likely to feel OK about dealing with other people'. The target was the airline's 12,000 customer-contact staff, but this was soon extended to include support staff, highlighting the concept of 'internal' and 'external' customers. 150 staff from every level took part – baggage-handlers mixing with Concorde pilots, engineers with marketing managers.

Aimed at helping line workers and managers understand the service nature of the airline industry, it was intended to challenge the prevailing wisdom about how things were to be done at BA. But PPF also signalled to the workforce the attitude and intentions of BA's management. It represented a considerable investment of time and money, not least by the chief executive and his directors, one of whom appeared to round off every event with talk about their vision for the airline in the future.

A key element of PPF was that staff also became actively involved in developing ideas for improving customer service.

Customer First Teams, using the techniques of quality circles, were formed in many departments. Task forces continue to be used to solve emerging problems, such as those resulting from the acquisition of British Caledonian Airlines.

Nick Georgiades' appointment as Human Resource Director in September 1984 signalled a new role for the Personnel Department. The change of name represented a more fundamental shift in the way the function was to operate to support the change process. All human-resource professionals went on an intensive programme which focused on consultancy skills in the context of organisational change. Administrative procedures hitherto associated with the personnel role were handed over to line management to free up human resources to act as change agents within the organisation.

The 1,400 managers themselves needed to adapt their style in this brave new world and week-long residential programme 'Managing People First' (MPF) was launched in 1985. This advocated a more open, visible and dynamic management style. The key themes were:

- Urgency (emanating from leaders not events)
- Vision (having the image of the cathedral while mixing the cement)
- Motivation (expect the best, catch someone doing it right)
- Trust (giving confidence to the individual to act alone, and spirit to the group to act together)
- Taking responsibility (i.e., 'I am in charge of my own behaviour')

MPF represented one element of a change strategy which became known as 'The Three Legged Stool' – without one leg the stool would collapse. The other two legs were a performance appraisal system and a performance-related pay system for all managers. These schemes were created to emphasise customer service and subordinate development.

While PPF and MPF focused on the individual, a third major corporate event was launched in November 1985 which emphasised the benefits of collaborative working. The programme, 'A Day in the Life', gave staff a better understanding of what the major departments did and helped break down the barriers which exist in large organisations. A key element of the programme was the appearance again of either the chief executive or one of the directors to show top-level commitment.

A number of internal BA structures and systems were changed. By introducing a new bonus scheme, for example, Georgiades demonstrated management's commitment to sharing the financial gains of BA's success. The opening of Terminal 4 at Heathrow Airport provided a more functional work-environment for staff. The purchase of Chartridge House as a permanent BA training centre permitted an increase in the integration of staff training and the new user-friendly Management Information Systems (MIS) to get the information they needed to do their jobs in a timely fashion.

During the refreezing phase, the continued involvement and commitment of BA's top management ensured that the changes became fixed in the system. People who clearly exemplified the new BA values were much more likely to be promoted, especially at higher management levels.

Attention was paid to BA's symbols as well – new, improved uniforms; refurbished aircraft; and a new corporate coat of arms with the motto 'We fly to serve'. A unique development was the creation of teams for consistent cabin-crew staffing, rather than the ad-hoc process typically used.

'To Be the Best' was launched in 1987, against the background of growing competition, and focused on the competitive threats facing the airline and the importance of achieving and sustaining excellence in service delivery.

BA's culture had been transformed from what BA managers described as 'bureaucratic and militaristic' to one that is 'service-oriented and market-driven'.

This cultural upheaval wasn't without its problems. For instance, many managers had trouble reconciling having to show care and concern for their people with delivering profit and pro-ductivity improvements with fewer resources. The success of this radical change process was put to the test when BA's next crisis came in February 1991. BA was forced to lose some 4,500 staff and stand down a further 2,000 to weather the economic and political storms created by recession and the Gulf War. This twin threat had the potential to destroy much of the commitment and loyalty built up during the 1980s.

The external pressures driving the cut-backs were understood as being beyond the control the BA's management. The subsequent decision to allow strong American competition into Heathrow with no *quid pro quo* for British carriers in the US domestic market served to rally staff around the company. Over the previous year the airline had become increasingly concerned about its uncompetitive cost base and had commissioned McKinsey's to advise on a process for carrying out a company-wide overhead value analysis to identify and implement widescale cost-savings.

This was the third time the airline had had to resort to redundancy measures to tackle over-manning. On the positive side, this meant that BA had the experience of managing the redundancy process. But the announcement was also likely to invoke memories of the 1983 reorganisation which was still referred to as the 'Night of the Long Knives'.

Past experience also influenced the way the severance scheme was to be used this time. As previously, it was to be voluntary, but it was now targeted at specific jobs and work groups, rather than a free-for-all, which resulted in the airline losing some of its talented and highly marketable individuals.

A key decision which influenced the reactions of the majority of the workforce who were not personally affected by the cuts was to transform BA's recruitment centre into an outplacement service. This was inspired by one of the basic customer-service principles: namely, the way you handle an individual passenger will be observed by all those passengers in the immediate vicinity and will affect their view of the company as a whole.

The Advice and Support Centre signalled the extent of BA's concern for its people in tough times. BA were seen to be offering both practical and emotional support to redundant staff. The fact that the service was available to people for up to six months after they had officially left BA was another sign of the company's level of commitment. BA's sensitivity in this redundancy exercise, far from representing a betrayal of corporate values, actually reinforced them more strongly.

This is what makes the sad saga of the 'dirty tricks' campaign against Virgin Airlines so mystifying. It appears that some of BA's staff became over-zealous and penetrated the customer data of their BA's rival, Virgin Airlines. They were accused of using this data to pressurise Virgin customers to switch to BA.

This debacle has cost the corporation millions of pounds in compensation to date, and also been a public relations disaster. So much so that it has threatened to undo all the good work of Lord King and Marshall.

The fact that such dirty tricks were allowed to flourish during this period puts a question mark over the calibre of senior management in key areas of operations. But another more disturbing element is that BA may have become so inward-looking during this time of transition that they underestimated the threat which Richard Branson's airline posed.

It also resulted in Lord King's departure from the helm on a particularly sour note. The fact that this sad episode blotted an otherwise exemplary book in BA's history is one thing, but what is perhaps more worrying for the long term is the admission by a senior BA executive that they under-estimated Richard Branson 'because he did not wear a suit'. This suggests that the change process within BA still has a long way to go.

It may be that BA's biggest problem now is not so much to manage further change but to manage the change that has already occurred. In other words, the people of BA have achieved significant change and success; now they must maintain what has been achieved while concentrating on continuing to be adaptable to changes in their external environment e.g. the further deregulation of Europe, their search for partnerships in the United States and their future response to Richard Branson and Virgin Airlines. Managing momentum may be more difficult than managing change.

Assignment Questions

Discuss the following:

1. Why did King and Marshall undertake a major exercise in empowerment?
2. What did they actually do to make the 'teams' within the organisation work as empowered teams?
3. How was the empowerment exercise conducted and was it successful?
4. What went wrong – as managers, what process of empowerment did they ignore?

Empowering Teams Exercise

Assignment

This exercise is designed for subgroups of ten people. Thus, in a class/group of 30 people there will be three subgroups. Each subgroup will be divided into three teams which together represent one advertising organisation.

The Top Team consists of two people, the Middle Team consists of three people, and the Bottom Team consists of five people. Each team has its own responsibilities, described below. You will be assigned to one of the three teams on a random basis.

The object of this exercise is to satisfy the customer. You should try, therefore, not only to deliver what is expected, but to actually exceed customer expectations. The customer is a distributor of new, cutting-edge products that have not yet become established in the marketplace. Your advertising organisation has been requested to create as many creative and exciting television commercials as you can for each product in this portfolio. The customer wants to choose among several different options for each product, so you need to generate an array of choices. At the end of the exercise, only one advertising organisation will be selected. The products in the customer's portfolio are:

■ A new kind of soft drink that contains fruit juice
■ A new kind of baby food formulation with extra vitamins
■ A new video game based on principles of chess
■ A new hand-held photocopying machine

- A new light bulb that lasts twice as long as regular bulbs
- A new kind of shampoo for grey hair that adds 'body'

Your task is to create, in written form, as many television commercials as you can for each product. You will be given 25 minutes. Your ideas will be evaluated by the customer, based on innovativeness, excitement, perceived effectiveness and cost. Your costs are associated with script writing, filming, actors and location. Using well-known personalities, lots of people, and exotic locations increases your costs.

Members of the Top Team have the following responsibilities:
- Task-assignments for organisation members
- Organisation design
- Reward and recognition system
- Control over production resources (paper, pens, Post-It notes)
- Determination of whether the product is of sufficient quality to be shown to the customer

Members of the Middle Team have the following responsibilities:
- Supervising the work of the Bottom Team
- Evaluating quality
- Serving as liaisons between the Top and Bottom Teams
- Carrying out assignments from the Top Team
- Determining whether the commercials are high, moderate or low cost
- Passing products to the Top Team

Members of the Bottom Team have the following responsibilities:
- Generating ideas for commercials
- Outlining the scripts
- Passing products to the Middle Team

At the end of the exercise, each organisation will be given three minutes to describe its products. Presentations, therefore, must be brief and to the point. The 'customer' will be other members of the class who will rate the product portfolio. Individuals may not evaluate their own organisation's products.

Each class member or 'customer' will complete a Customer Scoring Sheet from the Scoring Key at the end of the book (page 84) for each organisation. The scoring sheets will determine which organisation receives the highest point total. The organisation which obtains the highest score will be hired.

Assignment Questions

1. What principles of empowerment were most successful in this organisation?
2. What tendencies exist to maintain power differentials among teams?
3. What kinds of resistance to cooperation and teamwork did you experience?
4. What methods of organising work were most effective?
5. How effective was the delegation?
6. How could empowerment have been improved? What advice would you give others?

Skill Application

Application Activities for Empowering and Delegating

Suggested Further Assignments

1. Teach someone else (a fellow student, a colleague, your boss) how to empower others and delegate effectively. Use your own examples and illustrations.
2. Interview a manager about his or her empowerment practices. Try to determine what is especially effective, what doesn't work, what comes off as condescending and what motivates people to perform. Identify the extent to which the manager knows and uses the principles discussed in the Skill Learning section of this book.
3. Think of a situation you now face with which you would like some help. It may be a task you want to accomplish, a tough decision you need to make or a team you want to form. Make sure you think of something that requires the involvement of other people. Write down specific things you can do to empower other people to help you. How can you help them do what they want to do, and at the same time have them do what you want them to do?
4. Arrange a meeting with a manager who is not very good at empowerment. As a student who has learned about and practised empowerment and delegation, share what you have learned and offer suggestions which could help this manager improve.

Application Plan and Evaluation

The intent of this exercise is to help you apply your skills in a real-life, out-of-class setting. Now that you have become familiar with the behavioural guidelines that form the basis of effective skill-performance, you will improve most by trying out those guidelines in an everyday context. Unlike a classroom activity, in which feedback is immediate and others can assist you with their evaluations, this skill application activity is one you must accomplish and evaluate on your own. There are two parts to this activity. Part 1 helps prepare you to apply the skill. Part 2 helps you evaluate and improve on your experience. Be sure to write down answers to each item. Don't short-circuit the process by skipping steps.

Part 1 – Planning

1. Write down the two or three aspects of this skill that are most important to you. These may be areas of weakness, areas you most want to improve, or areas that are most salient to a problem you face currently. Identify the specific aspects of this skill that you want to apply.
2. Now identify the setting or the situation in which you will apply this skill. Establish a plan for performance by actually writing down a description of the situation. Who else will be involved? When will you do it? Where will it be done?
3. Identify the specific behaviours you will engage in to apply this skill. Operationalise your skill performance.
4. What are the indicators of successful performance? How will you know you have been effective? What will indicate that you have performed competently?

Part 2 – Evaluation

5. After you have completed your implementation, record the results. What happened? How successful were you? What was the effect on others?
6. How can you improve? What modifications can you make next time? What will you do differently in a similar situation in the future?
7. Looking back on your whole skill practice and application experience, what have you learned? What has been surprising? In what ways might this experience help you in the long term?

Scoring Key

Effective Empowerment and Delegation

To find your score for each skill area, add your rating scores together for the relevant questions.

Skill area	Question Nbr	Assessment Pre-	Post-
Personal mastery experiences	1, 2	_____	_____
Modelling	3, 4	_____	_____
Providing support	5, 6	_____	_____
Arousing positive emotions	7, 8	_____	_____
Providing information	9, 10	_____	_____
Providing resources	11, 12	_____	_____
Organising teams	13, 14	_____	_____
Creating confidence	15, 16	_____	_____
Delegating work	17–26	_____	_____
TOTAL SCORE		_____	_____

To assess how well you scored on this instrument, compare your scores to two comparison standards:

- Compare your score against the maximum possible (156).
- Compare your scores with the scores of other students in your class.

Personal Empowerment Assessment

For each skill area below, total your rating score for the four questions and divide by four to calculate the mean.

Skill area	Question Nbrs	Mean (Total/4)
Self-efficacy (competence)	2, 7, 12, 17	_____
Self-determination (choice)	3, 8, 13, 18	_____
Personal control (impact)	4, 9, 14, 19	_____
Meaningfulness (value)	1, 6, 11, 16	_____
Trust (security)	5, 10, 15, 20	_____

To determine the extent to which you are empowered, compare your scores to those of approximately 3,000 middle managers in manufacturing and service organisations:

Skill area	Mean	Top 1/3	Bottom 1/3
Self-efficacy	5.76	>6.52	<5.00
Self-determination	5.50	>6.28	<4.72
Personal control	5.49	>6.34	<4.64
Meaningfulness	5.88	>6.65	<5.12
Trust	5.33	>6.03	<4.73

Customer Scoring Key

Empowering Teams Exercise

Dimension	Score				
	Terrific		OK		Poor
Innovativeness	5	4	3	2	1
Excitement	5	4	3	2	1
Probable effectiveness	5	4	3	2	1
Number of commercials	5	4	3	2	1
Overall quality	5	4	3	2	1
	Great bargain		OK		Too high
Cost	5	4	3	2	1

TOTAL SCORES

Organisation 1   ——

Organisation 2   ——

Organisation 3   ——

Organisation 4   ——

Organisation 5   ——

Organisation 6   ——

Organisation 7   ——

Glossary

Creative problem-solving	A process where issues are approached from directions not entirely dictated by precedent or logic.
Diagnostic surveys	Questionnaires used to establish the state of knowledge or understanding of the reader.
Empowerment	A process whereby people are given authority in balance with their responsibilities whereby they can accomplish their set objectives using their own balance of initiative and discretion.
Modelling	Setting an example for others to copy. Thus managers wanting to spread an 'open door' policy in their organisations would have their own doors open to all staff.
'Pull' strategy	A way of changing the behaviour of others based on influence as opposed to coercion.
'Push' strategy	A way of changing the behaviour of others by some form of coercion.
Self-actualisation	In the Maslow Hierarchy of Needs the fulfilment of physiological needs is seen as the base and self actualisation as the pinnacle. Perhaps with some reference to Zen, self actualisation is seen as a state when personal fulfilment has been achieved.
Small wins	Using a 'small wins' strategy, the total 'project' or 'job' is divided into small steps and these are used as places for success or failure to be discussed.
Supportive communication	Communication that provides the necessary information for the task but at minimum maintains good personal relations between the parties involved.
Theory X	McGregor proposed two polarities in the way manager's perceived the starting position of their workforce. In Theory X, people are out for what they can get and need to be coerced to work. In theory Y, work is part of the human condition and given the right conditions, people are reasonable and will contribute according to their abilities and skills.
Threat-rigidity	A behaviour where the response to a threat of change is characterised by extreme conservatism. The ostrich 'head in the sand' would be an extreme case.

References

Abrahams, P. Management: Creating cracks in the layers. *Financial Times*, 5 April 1993.

Alday, R. J. & Brief, A. P. *Task design and employee motivation*. Glenview, Ill: Scott Foresman, 1979.

Alinsky, S. D. *Rules for radicals: A pragmantic primer for realistic radicals*. New York: Vintage Books, 1971.

Alloy, L. B., Peterson C., Abrahamson, L. Y. & Seligman, M. E. P. Attributional style and the generality of learned helplessness. *Journal of Personality and Social Psychology*, 46, 681-687, 1984.

Anderson, C., Hellreigel, D. & Slocum, J. Managerial response to environmentally induced stress. *Academy of Management Journal*, 20, 260-272, 1977.

Ashby, R. *Design for the brain*. London: Science Paperbacks, 1956.

Averill, J. R. Personal control over aversive stimuli and its relationship to stress. *Psychological Bulletin*, 80, 286-303, 1973.

Bandura, A. Self-efficacy: Toward a unifying theory of behavioral change. *Psychological Review*, 84, 191-215, 1977.

Bandura, A. *Social foundations of thought and action: A social cognitive theory*. Englewood Cliffs, N. J.: Prentice-Hall, 1986.

Bandura, A. Human agency in social cognition theory. *American Psychologist*, 44, 1175-1184, 1989.

Barber, B. *The logic and limits of trust*. New Brunswick, N.J.: Rutgers University Press.

Bennis, W. & Nanus, B. *Leaders: The strategies for taking charge*. New York: Harper and Row, 1985.

Bernard, C. I. *The functions of the executive*. Cambridge: Harvard University Press, 1938.

Block, P. *The empowered manager: Positive political skills at work*. San Francisco: Jossey-Bass, 1987.

Bookman, A. & Morgan, S. *Women and the politics of empowerment*. Philadelphia: Temple University Press, 1988.

Bramucci, R. *A factorial examination of the self-empowerment construct*. Ph.D. dissertation, University of Oregon, 1977.

Brehm, J. W. *Response to loss of freedom: A theory of psychological reactance.* New York: Academic Press, 1966.

Byham, W. C. *Zapp! The lightning of empowerment.* London: Century Business, 1991.

Cameron, K. S., Freeman, S. J. & Mishra, A. K. Best practices in white-collar downsizing: Managing contradictions. *Academy of Management Executive*, 1991.

Cameron, K. S., Freeman, Sarah J. & Mishra, A. K. *Organization downsizing and redesign.* In *Organizational change and design*, edited by G. P. Huber and W. Glick. New York: Oxford University Press, 1993.

Cameron, K. S., Kim, M. U. & Whetten, D. A. Organizational effects of decline and turbulence. *Administrative Science Quarterly*, 32, 222-240, 1987.

Cameron, K. S., Whetten, D. A. & Kim, M. U. Organizational dysfunctions of decline. *Academy of Management Journal*, 30, 126-138, 1987.

Cameron, K. S., Whetten, D. A., Kim, M. U. & Chaffee, E. E. The aftermath of decline. *Review of Higher Education*, 10, 215-234, 1987.

Coch, L. & French, J. R. P. Overcoming resistance to change. *Human Relations*, 11, 512-532, 1948.

Conger, J. A. Leadership: The art of empowering others. *Academy of Management Executive*, 3, 17-24, 1989.

Conger, J. A. & Kanungo, R. N. The empowerment process. *Academy of Management Review*, 13, 471-482, 1988.

Coonradt, C. A. *The game of work.* Salt Lake City: Shadow Mountain Press, 1985.

DeCharms, R. Personal causation and perceived control. In *Choice and perceived control*, edited by L. C. Perlmuter and R. A. Monty. Hillsdale, N. J.: Erlbaum, 1979.

Deci, E. L. & Ryan, R. M. The support of autonomy and control of behavior. *Journal of Personality and Social Psychology*, 53, 1024-1037, 1987.

Deci, E. L., Connell, J. P. & Ryan, R. M. Self-determination in a work organization. *Journal of Applied Psychology*, 74, 580-590, 1989.

Deutsch, M. *The resolution of conflict: Constructive and destructive processes.* New Haven: Yale University Press, 1973.

DiClemente, C. C. *Perceived efficacy in smoking cessation.* Paper presented at the annual meeting of the American Association for the Advancement of Science, Los Angeles, 1985.

Drucker, P. The coming of the new organization. *Harvard Business Review* (January-February), 1988.

Eisenhart, K. M. & Galunic, D. C. Renewing the strategy-structure-performance paradigm. *Research in Organizational Behavior*, 15, 1993.

Emery, F. E. & Trist, E. L. The casual texture of organisational environments. *Human Relations*, 18, 21-32, 1965.

Freire, P. & Faundez, A. *Learning to question: A pedagogy of liberation.* New York: The Continuum Publishing Company, 1989.

Gambetta, D. *Trust: Making and breaking cooperative relations.* Cambridge, Mass.: Basil Backwell, 1988.

Gecas, V. The social psychology of self-efficacy. *Annual Review of Sociology*, 15, 291-316, 1989.

Gecas, V., Seff, M. A. & Ray, M. P. *Injury and depression: The mediating effects of self concept.* Paper presented at the Pacific Sociological Association Meetings, Las Vegas, 1988.

Gennill, G. R. & Heisler, W. J. Fatalism as a factor in managerial job satisfaction. *Personnel Psychology*, 25, 241-250, 1972.

Gibb, J. R. & Gibb, L. M. Role freedom in a TORI group. In *Encounter theory and practice of encounter groups*, edited by A. Burton. San Francisco: Jossey-Bass, 1969.

Golembiewski, R. T. & McConkie, M. The centrality of trust in group processes. In *Theories of group processes*, edited by Gary Cooper. New York: Wiley, 1975.

Greenberger, D. B. & Stasser, S. The role of situational and dispositional factors in the enhancement of personal control in organizations. *Research in Organizational Behavior*, 13, 111-145, 1991.

Greenberger, D. B., Stasser, S., Cummings, L. & Dunham, R. B. The impact of personal control on performance and satisfaction. *Organizational Behavior and Human Decision Processes*, 43, 29-51, 1989.

Hackman, J. R. & Oldham, G. R. *Work design.* Reading, Mass.: Addison Wesley, 1980.

Hammer, H. & Champy, J. *Re-engineering the corporation.* London: Nicholas Brealey, 1993.

Hammer, T. H. & Vardi, Y. Locus of control and career self-management among nonsupervisory employees in industrial settings. *Journal of Vocational Behavior*, 18, 13-29, 1981.

Handy, C. *The age of unreason.* London: Arrow, 1990.

Handy, C. *The empty raincoat.* London: Hutchinson, 1994.

Harter, S. Effectance motivation reconsidered: Toward a developmental model. *Human Development*, 21, 34-64, 1978.

Herriot, P. & Pemberton, C. *New deals: the revolution in managerial careers.* Wiley, 1995.

Huber, G. P. *Managerial decision making.* Glenview, Ill.: Scott Foresman, 1980.

Kahn, W. A. Psychological conditions of personal engagement and disengagement at work. *Academy of Management Journal*, 33, 692-724, 1990.

Kanter, R. M. Commitment and social organization: A study of commitment mechanisms in utopian communities. *American Sociological Review*, 33, 499-517, 1968.

Kanter, R. M. *The change masters.* New York: Simon & Schuster, 1983.

Katzenbach, J. R. & Smith, D. K. *The wisdom of teams.* Massachusetts: Harvard Business Press, 1993.

Langer, E. J. *The psychology of control.* Beverly Hills: Sage, 1983.

Langer, E. J. & Rodin, J. The effects of choice and enhanced personal responsibility. *Journal of Personality and Social Psychology*, 34, 191-198, 1976.

Lawrence, P. & Lorsch, J. *Organizations and environments.* Homewood, Ill.: Irwin, 1967.

Lawler, E. E. *The ultimate advantage: Creating the high involvement organization.* San Francisco: Jossey-Bass, 1992.

Leana, C. R. Power relinquishment versus power sharing: Theoretical clarification and empirical comparison on delegation and participation. *Journal of Applied Psychology*, 72, 228-233, 1987.

Locke, E. A. & Schweiger, D. M. Participation in decision making: One more look. *Research in Organizational Behavior*, 1, 265-340, 1979.

Luhmann, N. *Trust and power.* New York: Wiley, 1979.

Manz, C. C. & Sims, H. *Super-leadership: Teaching others to lead themselves.* Englewood Cliffs, N.J.: Prentice-Hall, 1989.

Marx, K. *Early Writings.* Edited and translated by T. B. Bottomore. New York: McGraw-Hill.

Maslow, A. *Eupsychian Management.* Homewood, Ill.: Irwin, 1965.

McClellend, D. *Power: The Inner Experience.* New York: Irvington, 1975.

Mishra, A. K. *Organizational response to crisis: The role of mutual trust and top management teams.* Ph.D. dissertation, University of Michigan, 1992.

Neufeld, R. W. J. & Thomas, P. Effects of perceived efficacy of a prophylactic controlling mechanism on self-control under painful stimulation. *Canadian Journal of Behavioral Science*, 9, 224-232, 1977.

Newman, W. H. & Warren, K. *The process of management.* Englewood Cliffs, N.J.: Prentice-Hall, 1977.

Nielson, E. H. Empowerment strategies: Balancing authority and responsibility. In *Executive Power*, edited by S. Scrivastiva et al. San Francisco: Jossey-Bass, 1986.

Organ, D. & Greene, C. N. Role ambiguity, locus of control, and work satisfaction. *Journal of Applied Psychology*, 59, 101-112, 1974.

Ozer, E. M. & Bandura, A. Mechanisms governing empowerment effects: A self-efficacy analysis. *Journal of Personality and Social Psychology*, 58, 472–486, 1990.

Peters, T. *Liberation management*. Basingstoke: Macmillan, 1992.

Peters, T. & Waterman, R. *In search of excellence*. London: Harper Collins, 1982.

Preston, P. & Zimmerer, T. W. *Management for supervisors*. Englewood Cliffs, N.J.: Prentice-Hall, 1978.

Rappoport, J., Swift, C. & Hess, R. *Studies in empowerment: Steps toward understanding and action*. New York: Haworth Press, 1984.

Rose, S. M. & Black, B. L. *Advocacy and empowerment: Mental health care in the community*. Boston: Routledge and Kegan Paul, 1985.

Rothbaum, F., Weisz, J. R. & Snyder, S. S. Changing the world and changing the self: A two-process model of perceived control. *Journal of Personality and Social Psychology*, 42, 5–37, 1982.

Runyon, K. E. Some interaction between personality variables and management style. *Journal of Applied Psychology*, 57, 288–294, 1973.

Sashkin, M. *A manager's guide to participative management*. New York: American Management Association, 1982.

Sashkin, M. Participative management is an ethical imperative. *Organizational Dynamics*, 12, 4–22, 1984.

Schneider, J. A. & Agras, W. W. A cognitive behavioral treatment of bulimia. *British Journal of Psychiatry*, 146, 66–69, 1985.

Schwalbe, M. L. & Gecas, V. Social psychological consequences of job-related disabilities. In *Work experience and psychological development through life span*, edited by J. T. Mortimer and K. M. Borman. Boulder, Colo.: Westview, 1988.

Seeman, M. & Anderson, C. S. Alienation and alcohol. *American Sociological Review*, 48, 60–77, 1983.

Seligman, M. E. P. *Helplessness: On depression, development, and death*. San Francisco: Freeman, 1975.

Semler, R. *Maverick*. Century: London, 1993.

Sewell, Carl. *Customers for life*. New York: Pocket Books, 1990.

Solomon, B. B. *Black empowerment: social work in oppressed communities*. New York: Columbia University Press, 1976.

Spreitzer, G. M. *When organizations dare: The dynamics of individual empowerment in the workplace*. Ph.D. dissertation, University of Michigan, 1992.

Strauss, G. Some notes on power equalization. In *The Social Science of Organizations*, edited by H. Levitt. Englewood Cliffs, N.J.: Prentice-Hall, 1963.

Staples, L. H. Powerful ideas about empowerment. *Administration on Social Work*, 14, 29–42, 1990.

Staw, B., Sandelands, L. & Dutton, J. Threat-rigidity effects in organizational behavior: A multilevel analysis. *Administrative Science Quarterly*, 26, 501-524, 1981.

Sye, J. & Connolly, C. *Sporting Body, Sporting Mind*. Cambridge UP, 1984.

Thomas, K. W. & Velthouse, B. A. Cognitive elements of empowerment: An interpretive model of intrinsic task motivation. *Academy of Management Review*, 15, 666-681, 1990.

Urwick, L. *Elements of administration*. New York: Harper and Brothers, 1944.

Vogt, J. F. & Murrell, K. L. *Empowerment in organizations*. San Diego: University Associates, 1990.

Vroom, V. H. & Jago, A. G. Decision making as social process: Normative and descriptive models of leader behavior. *Decision Sciences*, 5, 743-769, 1974.

Vroom, V. H. & Yetton, P. W. *Leadership and decision making*. Pittsburgh: University of Pittsburgh Press, 1973.

Weick, K. E. *The social psychology of organizing*. Reading, Mass.: Addison-Wesley, 1979.

White, R. W. Motivation reconsidered: The concept of competence. *Psychological Review*, 66, 297-333, 1959.

Zand, D. E. Trust and managerial problem solving. *Administrative Science Quarterly*, 17, 229-239, 1972.

Zimmerman, M. A. Taking aim on empowerment research: On the distinction between individual and psychological conceptions. *American Journal of Community Psychology*, 18, 169-177, 1990.

Zimmerman, M. A. & Rappaport, J. Citizen participation, perceived control, and psychological empowerment. *American Journal of Community Psychology*, 16, 725-750, 1988.

Index

5